ENZO

The Adventure of a Friendship

Emilio Bonicelli

Foreword by Lodovico Balducci

Hamilton Books
A member of
The Rowman & Littlefield Publishing Group
Lanham · Boulder · New York · Toronto · Plymouth, UK

Italian edition copyright © 2009 by
Casa Editrice Marietti S.p.A.—Genova-Milano

English translation copyright © 2011 by
Hamilton Books
4501 Forbes Boulevard
Suite 200
Lanham, Maryland 20706
Hamilton Books Acquisitions Department (301) 459-3366

Estover Road
Plymouth PL6 7PY
United Kingdom

All rights reserved

British Library Cataloging in Publication Information Available

Library of Congress Control Number: 2011932290
ISBN: 978-0-7618-5649-8 (clothbound : alk. paper)
ISBN: 978-0-7618-5650-4 (paperback : alk. paper)
eISBN: 978-0-7618-5651-1

And seek out day by day the faces of the saints, in order that you may rest upon their words.
                                        The Didachè

Table of Contents

Foreword to the English Edition
Enzo: An Act of Faith *by Lodovico Balducci*   vii

Introduction *by Giancarlo Cesana*   ix

The Operating Room   1

Chapter One: A Friend   17

Chapter Two: The Encounter   27

Chapter Three: A Father, Because He Was a Son   37

Chapter Four: *Sacrum facere*   45

Chapter Five: Face to Face with Destiny   53

Historical Information   65

The Enzo Piccinini Foundation   67

The Amistad Group   71

Acknowledgements   73

Foreword to the English Edition
Enzo: An Act of Faith

An act of faith is the ultimate manifestation of human freedom. By giving a unique sense to each individual history, an act of faith is the choice to belong to history and to make history. It embraces truths that one cannot fully understand, based on the authority of the person that professes and lives them. The root of my own religious faith may be found in my encounter with two Catholic priests that at different times preserved my life from self-destruction. The first convinced me not to commit suicide at age 16. The second allowed me to recognize that I was being held hostage by a personal relationship that prevented my own growth as a physician and as a person. I learned that they knew me and could judge what was good for me better than I myself could, because they loved me with unconditional love. This sprouted from a faith whose content I could not fully understand but which I found worth exploring as a source of meaning for my life, as the sun that alone could have dissipated the fog of my confusion.

The crisis of values that plagues our society may be attributed to the lack of opportunity for committing oneself in an act of faith, due to a culture in which relativism is lived as synonymous with freedom. In a culture that spurns trust the testimony of Enzo Piccinini represented a beacon of certitude, founded on friendship inspired by *agape*, the highest form of love.

My friendship with Enzo Piccinini also represented one of those rare experiences that lead to an act of faith. I did not know why Enzo pursued me so insistently after our first encounter, an encounter which I had judged to be lukewarm at best. I expressed to him my reservations about Communion and Liberation and did not conceal my acquaintances with and my appreciation of people who had been very critical of the Movement. Though I had turned down many an invitation to visit him in Bologna, he eventually succeeded in getting me there to give a conference and to share a meal with his friends. Then I could not help but be impressed by the school of hepatobiliary surgery he had built, despite a medical system that discouraged innovation and was suspicious of initiative. Enzo had created a center of excellence by visiting at his own expense and on his own time the most prestigious surgical departments of America and

Europe and by encouraging his followers to do the same. He resisted the temptation to build a personal empire because he lived his profession as a service inspired by a love that had infected his assistants and his students. That love supported the joy that permeated the actions of Enzo and his coworkers and that was also contagious. Once again, unconditional love inspired by faith had allowed me to find what was good for me despite myself; once again the contents of that faith were worth exploring.

Enzo's life itself had been turned around by an act of faith. Prior to meeting don Giussani he had tried to find a home in some of the most leftist movements that shook Italian society in the so called "lead years" (1968–1975). An act of faith in Giussani harnessed the forces underlying his rebellion against mediocrity and social injustice and transformed them into an indomitable creative force substantiated by love that promoted effective and important social changes. His professional and personal life has been an ongoing act of faith in love, whether he put his reputation at risk in performing a difficult procedure to save a human life despite the contrary advice of his colleagues, or whether he engaged tirelessly in raids across the Atlantic to support the mission of his sister in Venezuela, to hearten the communities of Communion and Liberation around the USA, and to spend some happy hours with his many friends.

Though this book is entitled "the adventure of a friendship" I highlighted the role of love in Enzo's testimony. Four ancient Greek words are translated as love in modern English: *eros,* that is, sexual passion; *filia,* that is, friendship; *eusebeia,* that is, the mutual affection of children and parents, and *agape,* that is, the unconditional form of love, the love that only wishes what is good for the person being loved. Enzo witnessed *agape* in all aspects of his life. In his testimony *agape* was the source of professional excellence and of personal joy, a joy that not even his untimely and tragic death could quench.

Lodovico Balducci
Program leader of Senior Adult Oncology at Moffitt Cancer Center and
Professor of Oncologic Sciences at the University of South Florida College of Medicine

Introduction

What can I say about Enzo and about the many people I have loved who are no longer here with us? Their lives are a promise.

Enzo was so intense and present that he scattered the darkness of death. As a consequence, death could do nothing to our memory of him or of his life-giving work. We are surrounded by his children, that is, by those who found life through him, who through him found the positive affirmation of a meaning for everything that exists. So it is not over and gone, not over and gone at all. Enzo's presence is not over and gone. Without his presence, we would understand much less about who we are; without his presence, a stable part of our world would be gone; without his presence, he himself could never have existed. His presence, in fact, is a communication of Being, of His eternity.

Enzo loved Father Giussani very much, and he was loved back in the same way. They were much alike in temperament, but most importantly there was their common passion about the discovery of Christ, their discovery of the human face of God, of Him who rebuilt, and who will rebuild in a definitive way even the weakness of the flesh. Joy arising from the God who is mercy was the experience that grounded the connection between Enzo and me, as we were both aware that at the deepest level, everything has been given to us, especially the possibility of belonging to a place of life, which is what the Movement is.

When I think of Enzo, what comes to mind is him and me surrounded by all of us, by those who are here and those who seem not to be here anymore. In the meantime, by the effect of their presence, we understand that they are here even more than before. When we say, as Father Giussani used to say, that our companionship is a friendship being guided to Destiny, Enzo appears to me as a clear guide, with no hesitation, because he gave his life for the work of Someone else. Because of this Someone who makes all of us, he is waiting for us.

In closing, I remember his family: Fiorisa, Chiara, Maria, Pietro, and Anna Rita. They too are protagonists of his greatness, having been made out of it, and, especially in the case of Fiorisa, having had a part in making it.

Giancarlo Cesana

The Operating Room

It was hard to find a surgeon like him. He never gave up. He had the fearless and curious eyes of a child. He knew how to risk when others held back. When a patient turned to him, he took that person to heart and never abandoned him, even when there was nothing more to do from the surgical point of view. But if there was even the least possibility of a solution, he would doggedly pursue it.

So one Sunday morning a friend telephoned him from a large hospital in Milan. "Listen, Enzo," he began.

Paola[1] was ill. Doctors would stop by her bed at visitation time, palpating her abdomen and looking at her ugly, seeping wounds. They looked over the latest charts, shut their folders and walked on without saying a word, silent and evasive even when someone tried to chase them down and question them in the hallways. They would not freely speak of her case even among themselves. Meanwhile, Paola grew worse, had no strength, and felt sharper and more frequent pain, as days passed by with no resolution.

They had already operated on her twice in the past month. Her first surgery had been difficult, with many unforeseen complications. Then Paola took a turn for the worse, and they had to reopen her for emergency surgery. Now they were all silent. She was sick, but no one wanted to operate a third time, risking yet another failure. Better to let nature take its course.

"Listen, Enzo, you, at least, might be willing to try something for her. Please think about it. I'm afraid everyone here has given up on her as a lost cause."

Enzo was stuck. The faculty of medicine at the University of Bologna was in the process of taking decisive steps toward his university career. In the next few weeks he had to pass an examination, and the chief surgeon of the large and well known hospital in Milan, where Paola was hospitalized, was a member of the committee that would evaluate him.

---

1. *In this story taken from an episode of Enzo Piccinini's life, people's names have been changed out of respect for privacy, except for those of Enzo and Father Luigi Giussani.*

"What am I supposed to do?" wondered Enzo. "Go against a member of the examining board?" Then he blurted out a tentative response to get him out of his bind. "Look, the hospital where Paola is staying is one of the most qualified in Italy. They are very good."

"Yes, but Paola is fading fast. At least come to see her."

* * *

On Monday morning Enzo crossed the threshold of the hospital in Milan.

"Doctor Piccinini, what are you doing here?"

"I'm here to see a friend staying in your hospital. She's in serious condition. I would like to visit her. And how are you?"

For Paola, Enzo's visit was a source of comfort after days and days of anguish. Some time back she had listened to him giving a presentation during a conference and she had been impressed by his passion and how he had talked about himself and his profession as a surgeon in concrete terms, not resorting to platitudes.

Enzo showed concern as he visited her, along with one of the doctors from the hospital.

"Does it hurt here?"

"And how about here?"

He palpated gently and with practiced hand around her wounds that were refusing to heal.

He carefully read and reread her medical record, then went with the accompanying physician to talk with the rest of the hospital staff.

Eventually he came back and sat beside her bed.

"It's about time," thought Paola. "A doctor who has the courage to spend some time with me." This gesture had given her confidence: here was someone looking her in the eyes, taking an interest in her and speaking to her.

"Something's not right," Enzo began. "My colleagues here have done everything possible, but obviously there is something that they are not picking up on. You have to let me think about it. I need some time to consider the different elements and try to understand the situation. I will call you to let you know. You can count on it."

"Thanks," Paola said simply, and it was a heartfelt thanks. Finally a doctor was telling her what she had been feeling for days: "Something's not right." Finally, here was a doctor who cared about her, who was looking for an answer that could save her.

"Thanks."

* * *

"What are you going to do?" Paola's friend asked, as she walked along with Enzo toward the exit doors of the hospital, adding, "You could have her come to Bologna."

"I need a little time to reflect. I'll let you know."

That thought stayed with Enzo on his return trip along the freeway to Bologna as he rode the accelerator, late for his afternoon lesson at the university. He stayed in the left lane, leaving the endless line of trucks passing one another on his right.

"Okay. So in Milan they seem to have done everything possible. And yet.... But how can I bring her here, into my department? How can I request a transfer from one of the leading institutes in Italy—where the head surgeon is one of the commissioners I'll be facing in my next exam? It's impossible. Only an idiot would do such a thing."

Deep in his thoughts, he telephoned his secretary to ask her to have some food ready in his office, so he could grab a bite before rushing into the classroom to teach.

Flashing his headlights to signal his presence to any cars that were moving slowly in the left lane, he called Marta to get a detailed account of the visits to the patients in his ward. "Does the lady from Cremona still have a fever? How can you not remember? Run to take her temperature. I'll call you back right away, five minutes from now."

He stepped on the accelerator as he spoke with his wife. "I'm coming back from Milan. In the afternoon I have a lecture, and then the meeting with the interns. Then the dinner meeting with the leaders of the university. See you at midnight, if you're still awake."

* * *

The lights went out in the ward at eleven thirty. In the bed next to hers, an elderly lady had already been asleep for fifteen minutes, breathing heavily. Every so often she would start to cough—a dry and insistent cough. Paola, however, was wide awake. Although she felt exhausted, she could not keep her eyes closed, due to the pain in her stomach, a certain restlessness in her legs, and the coughing fits of her new neighbor that seemed each time as if they were about to suffocate her. But more than anything, she kept thinking of Enzo's words: "I will let you know." She thought over and over again of the way he had looked at her. "Finally there is someone who still cares about me."

After over an hour, around midnight, her neighbor's coughing seemed to have subsided, and Paola herself was about to slip into sleep when she got an unexpected visit. A dark figure appeared in the doorway. The room was dim, and only when the figure was close to her bed did Paola recognize the nurse who at the beginning of the night shift had gone around to adjust medications.

"There is a telephone call for you."

"For me?"

"There is a doctor from Bologna who says he was here today and urgently needs to talk to you."

"Enzo?"

"Piccinini."

"Hello. It's me."

"Paola, how are you?"

"I still have pain, and some restlessness in my legs."

"I thought it over. I've looked at all the factors. I've made a decision. I would like to take you under my care."

"Really? This is the news I've been waiting for!"

"But there's a problem. It's preferable to care for you here in my hospital. I'm calling you before making an official request to find out what you think, how you feel about being transferred in your condition, considering the long journey."

"Yes Yes. I have no doubts. I would leave right now if I could. Right away."

"You know that it's not a simple situation. There are difficulties. To begin with, I will put you under observation to see if there is any room for action. We will watch you very carefully."

"If there is a chance?"

"If there is a chance, we'll find it. Count on it. And know that when you get here we will fight side by side every day, no matter happens. My colleagues and I will be at your side."

"Then I'm coming. When?"

"Tomorrow. For now, sleep—it's late. In fact, what were you doing still awake? What kind of nightlife do you have there in Milan?"

"Oh, come on! Well okay, I was listening to the symphony of my neighbor's coughing," Paola said with a smile, and it was the first time she had smiled in a long time.

"Good night."

"Good night."

* * *

The trip from Milan to Bologna was long. The ambulance drove slowly. At every bump, Paola felt sick. It was a quiet trip because of the nausea that was gripping her throat, and the nurse who sat beside her was a man of few words. Her pain and nausea grew as the ambulance exited the freeway and entered city traffic. With every brake a twinge, and a jab at every pothole. At one point Paola began to wonder if it was worth it, whether it would have been better to stay where she was. More than anything else she longed to be lying on a bed, to have something soft and stable under her.

At long last the ambulance stopped. The engine was turned off and the back doors opened. Paola was sick; her nausea turned to vomiting, and as her breathing became labored with the tension, her mind grew insistent with the question, "Was it worth it?" But then, as she lay on the gurney and was being pushed into the ward, her doubts suddenly vanished. Waiting for her there was not only the head nurse, but also Enzo with his team of young doctors. Paola's eyes filled with tears. They were all there for her, and they had already arranged appointments for radiology and lab work so that the necessary analyses would be ready by evening. There was no time to spare. For several hours Paola had no time to think until, exhausted, she fell asleep, despite her nausea, in her bed in the ward.

* * *

The next week was the hardest. Her pain continued to grow, and to the pain were added fits of vomiting. Paola could not fall asleep. Even at night she only dozed off from time to time, only to wake up again after a few minutes. Enzo went to visit her every day when his commitments in the operating room allowed him to, always followed by the group of young doctors. There was a striking unity and harmony among them. On each visit, Enzo asked Paola for any news about her physical condition. He would explain the symptoms that were showing up in that difficult situation, watching everything carefully, lifting her spirits.

In the early morning on the seventh day, Enzo showed up alone and sat down beside Paola's bed.

"How are you?"

"Bad," Paola said in a faint voice.

"We can't wait any longer. It would be dangerous. We would be taking the risk of acting too late. All the data we collected this week tell me that unless we operate, there is only one outcome for you, and that outcome is that you will die. But if we operate, it's not certain, it's not for sure, but there is a chance of success. There is a possibility that we can save you. I wanted to speak to you personally and frankly, to find out what you, what you think about it."

"If there's a chance, even if just a small one, if you see it, then I want to have the operation."

"Are you sure?"

"Yes."

"So let's plan for tomorrow."

"Tomorrow?"

"If you've made up your mind, all the data are telling me that it's better not to wait. We'll operate tomorrow."

* * *

It was seven o'clock in the morning when the nurses pushed the gurney into the operating room.

Paola was afraid. Her legs were shaking at the thought of being operated on again, with just one small chance of success. Her throat grew tight and she couldn't breathe well out of fear of the anesthesia. The same thing had happened before her other operations: drifting into sleep made her feel like she was dying. She was tormented by the thought of not waking up again.

Enzo had perceived her fear, and as he led the way into the operating room, he turned back, stopped the gurney, held her hand and smiled.

"Cheer up. Don't be afraid. This is not the dangerous part. Not under the knife. The dangerous part comes later. So don't worry: you will wake up and we'll see one another soon."

Paola felt relieved by that simple gesture, by the unexpected attention given to her, by that look, and by those words, and she finally breathed deeply.

"Someone's on the phone for you," added her friend, who had come to Bologna and who was now standing near her at the door of the operating room. "It's for you," and she held out her cell phone.

A little shaky, Paola took it, almost unable to speak.

"Hello."

"Paola."

"Hello."

"Paola."

On the other end of the line, her name was being pronounced by a hoarse, unmistakable voice.

"Don Giuss? Is that you?"

"Who else would it be? How are you feeling?"

"I'm afraid."

"Paola, do not be afraid. Your life will be saved because there is a people that is praying for you. We are all praying. We are asking insistently. We are not worthy of this grace, but you are."

"Thank you, don Giuss."

"Do not be afraid. When your recuperation is over, when you are healed, when all is past, when we meet, Christ will have drawn you a bit closer to himself and we will celebrate together."

* * *

As Paola slept on the operating table, Enzo looked at the X-ray plates while the nurses prepared her for surgery.

"It's a disaster."[2]

Enzo narrowed his eyes, frowned, and repeated, "It's a disaster. I've never seen so many fistulas in my life. Not only that, but you can't get anything from this X-ray. It's shocking. Yet if you look very carefully, see? You can see that there's a tiny space where we can save a bit of the intestine and reconnect here. Meanwhile, if we don't operate, Paola has no chance of survival."

Pietro was putting on latex gloves with the help of a nurse.

"A long procedure!"

---

2. Dialogues from the operating room are taken from episodes of Enzo Piccinini's life, as told by him and reported by his coworkers.

"Long, difficult, complicated," said Enzo. He paused thoughtfully, then added, "We'll have to stick with the reality, with what we find, observing it patiently. But there has to be a place where we can save a part of the intestine and reconnect it. There has to be, and we have to find it. So I will not give up."

Enzo hung up the X-ray plates and turned to the young colleague at his side, looking him in the eyes.

"Up in Milan, our colleagues there—you know them too."

"To be sure."

"People who know a whole lot about surgery."

"First class surgeons. What do they say?"

"Not to touch her, to leave her on a feeding tube. Period. Understand? If she makes it on her own, good; if nature helps her out, good for her; if not, she dies."

"They threw in the towel."

"Yeah. And they were insistent with me, too. Do not touch her! Do not touch her! If you put your hands on her, you will kill her. So I started thinking it over."

"They think we should wait and see."

"Wait for an impossible recovery and a guaranteed outcome."

"So we stand still and watch her die, Doctor? What a great plan! Why on earth would she have decided against it?" said the scrub nurse, a dark-skinned woman who, after gathering her hair under her cap, was putting on her mask.

"We talked a long time about her situation," said Enzo. "All the data we collected this week led me here. Her intestine is completely closed. We can't leave it be. Our colleagues said to keep our hands off it because it is too risky. But the data, the data, reality tells us that there is a tiny space for surgery here. And now it's up to us."

"I think it's the right decision."

"It will be a long operation. I mean look at this: it's a disaster."

"Doctor," said an older nurse, "I don't like long surgeries, and with you they always end up long. We have to talk about it. There are schedules, after all."

"I'm washing my hands," said Enzo loudly, interrupting the conversation so as not to trigger, in that moment, a white-hot debate with the old nurse.

He nodded to Pietro, with an eloquent look on his face. They went to the sink and continued to talk quietly to one another, while Enzo slipped on his mask, fastening the top strap on his head as usual.

"It couldn't have been an easy decision."

"You know, Pietro, these have been stressful days for me. I had to talk about it with Father Giussani, who knows Paola well."

"When did you talk with him?"

"Early yesterday morning. I called him on the phone and I told him that all the data are telling me that there's no time to lose, that we have to operate. But the doctors in Milan keep insisting that if I operate on her I will kill her.

'She's your friend,' I said. 'You've treated her like a daughter. So what should we do?'"

"What did he say?"

"You know, I'd already made a decision in my heart. We talked it over, and I said that the data are pointing me here. So I told him, 'I'm not asking for surgical advice, but with such a challenging decision, in taking such a risk, I need a judgment, some comfort. That's why I'm calling.'"

Enzo lifted his hands to let the water drip off before putting on his sterile gown and gloves.

"Giussani told me, 'You did the right thing in calling me, because you need some consolation for these decisions. It's right to want a judgment, because all the scientific truth in the world cannot provide the courage we need to fully face life. Consolation doesn't solve the problem, but the things that seem hardest are made clearer by companionship.'"

"You always say that we can't be alone."

"Right. Then he said these words that are like carved into me; I don't think I'll ever forget them: 'I don't know about dealing with people, but when it comes to God, we have to go ahead. Remember, freedom means not being afraid of failing, not because you're superficial, but because if you make your decisions based on fear of failure you no longer do anything.'"

Enzo looked at Pietro in silence for a few moments, and then he added in a somewhat louder voice, "I thought, 'That's right, if you're afraid of failing, you make your predictions and that's it.'"

"And then at some point you quit."

"But we have to go forward. When it comes to God, we have to go ahead."

"Doctor, what does that mean—that when it comes to God, we have to go ahead?" asked Anna, the scrub nurse, who had won Enzo's esteem because she was clever, precise, and very quick. She knew by intuition what the doctors were about to ask. She stayed on her feet for hours, next to the instrument table, without getting tired. True, she spoke every thought that passed through her head, but sometimes this helped to clarify matters.

"What does it mean?" Enzo replied. "It's fantastic. Look, Anna. The data are reality, and reality is not here by chance. There's somebody making it. If the data lead us here, if they brought us to the decision to operate, what can we do?"

"I don't know."

"How can't you know? We can't do otherwise. We have to stick with the reality, even if there are a thousand doubts, even if they tell you a thousand different things, even if there are many problems. Reality is not here by chance, and if the data lead us here, one thing is for sure. When it comes to God, we have to go ahead."

"I see. You look at it, and if that's how it is, you have to go ahead. So I'll get on my stand and hand you the instruments!"

* * *

Paola was lying on the operating table like Christ on the cross, with arms outstretched and tied down with safety straps. Her head, tilted slightly back, was hidden by a green drape. Her legs were bound by straps and her feet by compression stockings. Pietro sprinkled her abdomen with Betadine disinfectant with its characteristic reddish color. Monitoring and anesthesia equipment were already in operation, sending their rhythmic signals: buh-bum, beep, beep, beep, buh-bum.

Seated behind the table at Paola's head, the anesthesiologist monitored the figures running across the screen: pulse rate, blood pressure, breathing: buh-bum, buh-bum, buh-bum, beep, beep, beep, buh-bum.

As he moved in his swivel chair, he almost grazed Paola's head, with a respirator in her mouth and catheters threaded into her nose.

"Come on, Marta, you're late. What are you doing with your evenings, instead of going to bed early?" said Enzo as he turned to a young intern, who some time ago had come into his group of surgeons after doing her thesis with him. She was a young woman with a willful nature whom Enzo esteemed for her generosity.

"Doctor, do you want to take a guess who called me from his car yesterday while he was driving to tell me to get to the emergency room because one of our patients who had been released was rushed back in? Who do you think called me?"

"I might be able to guess."

"I thought you might."

"And you went in?"

"Of course."

"Thanks, Marta. There was no other way. I couldn't be there. I was coming from Bari and hadn't even made it to Pesaro."

"Yes, as always, you're right. Doctor. I was mad at first. But then I realized it had to be. I explained to the emergency room staff what we had done when we operated on him. If they hadn't had this information, things would have been tricky, I'm afraid."

"Thanks, Marta. But now, hurry up and get ready."

"I'm hurrying."

"In fact, before you wash your hands, put on some music, the kind that I like."

Marta walked to the metal container along the wall where there was a stereo CD player that Enzo had donated to the operating room so that work could be done while listening to good music. She opened a box containing a dozen CDs and chose what she knew to be Enzo's favorite. It was the first album of a rock band from San Francisco, famous at the time, called 4 Non Blondes. She selected the song "What's Up," and turned up the volume. Along with the melody the words rang out, "Twenty-five years and my life is still/ trying to get up that great big hill/ of hope for a destination." She liked the song too, and sometimes caught herself humming it in the ward.

Marta slipped on her mask, washed her hands and put on her scrubs. She went over to the table where Paola was lying, approaching the side across from Enzo so that she could watch and learn from what he was doing, and help him when called for.

"Be careful. Now we're going to make an incision here, like so."

"Pietro, you take the scissors and cut here. With precision. Try to follow me."

"Like this?"

"Just be careful: be mindful of structures; be mindful of tissues!"

"Like so?"

"Good. Lift."

"Clamp. Clamp."

Whoosh, whoosh, whoosh.

"Now we enter the peritoneum."

"Scalpel."

"Clamp. Clamp."

Enzo raised his arm, grabbed the handle of the operating lamp and swung it a little, lowering it so as to have more light.

"Gauze."

"Forceps."

"Clamp."

Anna stretched the gauze and cleaned the blades. The nurse picked up the bloody gauze and put it in a container so it could be counted later.

The sound of the anesthesia equipment was rhythmic and regular: dap, dap, dap, buh-bum, buh-bum, buh-bum, beep, beep, beep.

"Doctor," said Marta, as she leaned forward to see better, "I was a little late not only because of your phone call, but also because, before I came here, I visited the ward. I was worried about the lady from Cremona. She has a fever of 102."

"Make sure that they're giving her antibiotics."

"They've already begun."

"Orally?"

"Orally."

"It's better to do it intravenously—more effective. Once we're finished here in the operating room, go back to the ward and write the prescription. Make sure they give it to her intravenously."

"Of course."

"Let's widen the incision, or we won't be able to work in here."

"Marta, you work the retractor."

"Scalpel."

"No, not this one, the one for the incision. Anna, what's going on today? Where's your head?"

"I'm sorry, Doctor."

"Cut."

"Pad."

"Pad."
"Give me a damp patch."
"A little water."
"Lower the table."
"Just so."
"Clamp."
"Clamp."
Whoosh, whoosh, whoosh.
Enzo placed his hands in Paola's abdomen.
"Look here."
"Good Lord! From the X-rays it looked like a disaster. But here it's even worse. Everything's inflamed, all full of fistulas and adhesions."
"Give me the suction."
"Not this one; the other one."
"Suction. Suction. Just like that."
Enzo pulled out the blood-soaked gauze and the nurse went to put it in the container.
"And that makes twelve."
"Another large piece of gauze, damp."
"Cauterize here. Again."
Whoosh, whoosh.
"Everything's inflamed."
"It's all fragile."
"Give me the suction please."
"No. The cannula, the long one.
"Pietro, keep it here."
"Marta, pull the retractor back like this. Use more strength!"
"Good."
"Now I'm going to try to move very delicately."
"A syringe of water."
"Now it's all unknown territory."
"Look at this: we can't keep it."
"Not this either."
"Lift—just so, very slightly."
"Good Lord, it's all tangled."
"What inflammation!"
"Suction. Suction."
Whoosh, whoosh, whoosh.
"A little water."
"Marta, pull back more. Use more strength. I always say that you think like a man, but now you have to pull with the strength of a man."
"Okay. Like this, Doctor?"
"That's good."
"Doctor, I heard that you went to visit Marcello. I sure remember that feisty guy: he was always angry, but deep down, he was a good man."

"His wife called me and asked, 'Is my husband going to die?' I had to tell her, 'Yes.'"

"After six operations we couldn't open him up again."

"The pancreas is not a forgiving organ," interjected the scrub nurse, Anna.

"To be sure. The last operation let us spare him even worse pain and gave him a few more months to live, but it was impossible to stop the tumor. Unfortunately, Marcello had only a few days left to live. His wife asked, 'What should we do?' I told her, 'Tell him.' And his wife said, 'Do you think you could tell him?'"

"And so you went, Doctor?"

"I had promised him, when he was recovering from his first surgery: 'You can always count on me.'"

"Doctor, I'm not sure I would have had the courage to go," said Anna.

"Pietro, take the suction."

"Suction, Suction."

"Gauze."

"No, more."

"Marta, pull harder on the retractor."

"Like so?"

"More, more. Use more strength. Are you a man or aren't you?"

"I'm trying, Doctor."

"Doctor, how did you tell Marcello?"

"When I was at his house, in his bedroom, I sent everyone out and sat by his side. 'Look,' I said, 'things are complicated—very complicated. Anything could happen at any moment. You have to be ready.' At first his face was full of anger, but then I could see he was moved. His house is in the countryside, and there were drops of condensation on the windows. He told me, 'Look. We are like those drops. As long as there's a line of them, they stay in place. When the line collapses, they fall, and we're done for.'"

"And I said, 'Remember that the one holding that line is someone who loves us. It's not a bad thing to go back to him.' Then he started to cry. We hugged and said goodbye."

Bum, bum, bum, bum, beep, beep.

"Suction. Suction."

Whoosh, whoosh.

"Marta, pull the retractor."

"Look how it's attached. Right there!"

"It's one big fistula around the colon."

"These tissues are failing. They can't heal."

"There's an abscess here."

"A large piece of gauze."

"More gauze."

"Suction. Suction."

"If it keeps up like this, I don't know."

"Water."
"A syringe of water."
"Yesterday his wife called. She said he went to confession and took Communion. You see, Marta, we have to take our patients completely to heart and not give up on them, even in the face of death, because there is nothing more devastating than having cancer and not being able to have a human experience."
"Doctor, you certainly bring passion to what you do!"
"It's not because of me. It's because of the encounter I've had."
"Suction. Suction."
"A little water."
Whoosh, whoosh, whoosh, buh-bum, buh-bum.
"Look how it's attached here!"
"Clamp."
"Hold."
"Hold."
"This is out."
"There is another abscess here, with pus."
"Let's take a sample for biopsy."
"A large piece of gauze."
"Suction."
Enzo raised his arm and moved the lamp slightly so that the light would shine on the right spot. His latex glove was stained with blood, as was his coat.
"Hold on!"
"I've never seen anything like this before."
"If we make an incision here?"
"No! Look in back. Look in back! If we cut here, everything behind it will be closed up!"
"Move this loop."
"Let's at least make a preliminary incision; otherwise we can't get at it."
"Scalpel."
"Suction."
"Be careful of that artery."
"Cauterize."
"Hold."
"Hold."
"Go ahead."
"So taking others to heart, Doctor. But how do we do that?"
"Not like in America. The first time I worked there I was impressed, because everyone I came across in the ward asked me, 'How are you? How are you?' I was struck, and I thought, 'Finally! Someone is interested in me.' But when I stopped and started to give a real answer, they had already walked away. In other words, it was a formal gesture of courtesy, but they didn't care about me."
"How are you?"

"Everyone looked at me with a smile, but it was just manners. A true human relationship is something completely different."
"Suction."
"These cannulas are not working well."
"We have to replace them."
"Suction. Suction."
"Enough. Enough."
Whoosh, whoosh, bum, bum, bum, beep, beep.
"Damp gauze."
"Scalpel."
"No, the one for the incision."
"Anna, something's on your mind. How is your son?"
"That's exactly what's on my mind, Doctor. He's growing up, and he thinks in a totally different way from me. He's following ideas that I don't like. I'd like to tell him that things aren't like that, but that almost seems violent to me. Doctor, how can you have four children? Four! You're crazy."
"Anna, the problem is not how many children you have, but what you love. If you love someone, do you talk to him about what you read in the sports pages, or do you talk to him about yourself? Experience tells you that when you love someone, you talk him about yourself. If you love your children, you talk to them about yourself, about what you believe in. That's not violence. Loving somebody's freedom means offering a proposal, because freedom starts with having to say yes or no."
"Doctor, let's talk about this later."
"With pleasure. Meanwhile, I feel like having a good cigar."
"Here? It's not allowed!"
"I'll get to it once we've finished."
"Doctor, her pressure is dropping!"
Beep, beep, beep.

* * *

They had spent six hours in surgery. Paola's friend was sitting with other people in the waiting room beside the entrance to the operating room. Time kept passing and her worry kept growing, along with anguish. How can a procedure take so long? In her hand she was holding her rosary which she'd already used to pray through all the mysteries. She repeated the sorrowful mysteries many times, thinking of Paola under the knife.

At that moment, through the waiting room passed an intern, who was studying for a specialization in surgery with Enzo's group. He greeted her. They had met a week ago when Paola had first entered the hospital in Bologna. Paola's friend gathered her strength and asked, "Doctor, it's been six hours and I haven't had any news. Could you go in and see what's going on?"

"Wait for me here," replied the young man, and he entered a nearby room to put on slippers and then went into the operating room.

He came back after ten minutes.
Paola's friend stood up and anxiously went to meet him.
"The operation's still not over."
"She's still under the knife?"
"Yes, but it's going well. As far as possible, it's going well. They found a spot where they can reconnect. They took out everything they had to. But they found a spot where they can reconnect. It's going to work."
"But it's been six hours!"
"And it's going to take another two before they're done."

* * *

The first three days after the operation were critical for Paola, with continuing physical problems and a lot of unknowns about her chances for recovery. But then she felt that something was changing—for the better.
It was then that Enzo called Father Giussani.
"Don Giuss, Paola is doing surprisingly well."
"Why, did you have any doubts?"
"I was full of doubt."
"I want to thank you, because you have been the instrument of a miracle."
"Instrument of a miracle," thought Enzo at the end of the call. "That means that I have nothing to brag about, even if I saved her. But that is the basis of the Christian meaning of life, because the outcome does not depend on us, and this is what makes us free, not slaves of the results."

Chapter One
A Friend

The last time we saw one another, ten days before that terrible accident on the freeway, he gave me a goodbye hug. A big hug, as usual.

"It was extraordinary to see how his life was permeated with passion for Christ, even in the simplest and most everyday gestures—when eating lunch, talking together, discussing politics or our children's problems. There was someone else. He took you by the hand and walked on ahead with you. He opened new horizons in front of you. And so in his company, the day-to-day became exalted and sublime.

"Then a mysterious plan was fulfilled. And so one night, when he was returning from Milan, things got crazy on the road and his car slammed into an embankment. He was hurrying for his friends—to make the project of communion greater. And on that grassy embankment was his appointment, face to face, with the Lord. He ran on ahead. As always, he preceded us, consumed by a love that burned like a fire in his heart."

This is how I told the story of my last meeting with Enzo in my book *Ritorno alla vita* [*Back to Life*]. He had come to my house for supper with his daughter Anna Rita who was my daughter Caterina's classmate in their first year in the medicine and surgery department of the University of Bologna. Since then I have always had the desire to take up the thread of those words again, to expand that page and make it more fitting to the size of the friendship that we lived. Another book? Perhaps. More than a book. A living memorial for those who knew him. The gift of an encounter for those who were walking on different paths or were too young or too far away to have been warmed by the glow of his companionship. I kept this wish in my daily prayer and remembrance. So when I received an invitation from the Enzo Piccinini Foundation to prepare a text, a sort of biography, I gave in as if by momentum. It was what I myself had wanted. A book? Perhaps. More than a book, a journey in Enzo's company, and in the company of some of our friends.

My memory of Enzo is inextricably linked to a phrase that never grows old. He himself used to say of it, "I will always use that phrase." It began with a decisive question: *How can my life have unity?* Because having unity in life is the most important thing in the world. It can't be divided; it can't be split; it can't be reduced to a mosaic of juxtaposed situations. But Enzo pressed on: How can you unite sickness and health, free time and work, friendships and family? Is it possible? How is it done?

His answer: "Life has unity if you put your heart into what you do. I don't mean the heart as sentiment. I mean the irrepressible desire for happiness, goodness, truth, and justice. It's a desire you always have, and that by yourself you can never completely fulfill. Life can have unity if you put your whole heart, that is, your desire for complete happiness, into everything you do, whether easy situations or hard ones, fatigue or leisure, family or work. The heart is the irrepressible desire for truth, for beauty, for being loved and for loving. It's not a matter of philanthropy or of manners; it's not a problem of technique. But tomorrow morning, when I visit my patients in the hospital ward, if I put my heart into it, I will recognize in them the same desire that I have, and I will look at them differently."

To do this, however, you need something in your life bigger than you, so that you can belong to it and be accountable to it. It has to be something bigger, so that your desire for happiness is not extinguished by the outcome or by the lack of outcome, so that even the situations you don't understand can make sense. "It takes something bigger for us to be free."

But Enzo went on: Not even all of this is enough, because we cannot stand alone. "Even those with the loftiest intentions cannot do it. This bigger thing has to be something I experience, Someone who is present, Someone I can be accountable to—not just something that I feel and think, not just a Christian sentiment. It's like every time I close my eyes, I see the faces of my friends and I start over again."

"We can't be alone. We need a foothold; we need to belong. If you don't have something to refer to, so that your I is not adrift and unbound, so it has roots in faces and in stories, you can't make it. This is the real problem. Another reason we can't be alone is that if we are, we will lose the will to fight. Zest for life is not denied to those who make mistakes, but sooner or later it is denied to those who have no sense of the mystery in their lives, that is, of something bigger that is present, namely, a companionship that you can belong to."

"A real friendship."

Friendship. My journey in Enzo's company all begins with this word, with the intensity and depth with which he used it.

In Milan I talk about him with one of the people who was closest to him, Giancarlo. "He was a friend—God knows how much. We met almost every week for twenty years. He was a fantastic host. He liked to eat well and never once did I have to pay. He used to call me about every other day, often after midnight: 'How's it going?' At first I wouldn't know what to say, because it seemed to me that things were pretty much the same as the night before, but then we would talk. There was—there *is*—always something that was going well or not going so well. What impressed me about Enzo was his desire for judgment, for comparison. He had wonderful personal gifts, but he wanted to be corrected. This is a sign of belonging, of serving Someone else. We would argue with one another about everything, sometimes even bitterly, because we were certain that we shared a father, that is, Father Giussani, so it was clear, very clear, that the last word was not ours. Without the personal, intense relationship with Father Giussani, Piccinini and his life are incomprehensible."

Enzo spoke of Luigi Giussani[1] as a father, a father in the most authoritative sense of the term: a father who would challenge you, with no flattery; someone to refer to so that life could be sustained. And the challenge that came from him was hard and decisive, with no beating around the bush.

"For his part," says Giancarlo, "Father Giussani thought of him as a son. They shared a similar character and temperament, like two partners in crime. I was amazed how Enzo managed to hold everything together: working as a surgeon, which is a very demanding profession, along with devoting time to his family and the Movement.[2] His life had a profound unity. Everything served the same purpose."

Giancarlo shows me an article he wrote in memory of Enzo which appeared in the magazine *Traces*[3] in June of 1999. I read this sentence: "We were about the same age, sons of the university, a little ashamed of being leaders. Yet by reason of age and history, with no pretenses, we felt like fathers of the university students. It was no game. We used to talk about family, work, the Movement. The problem was not doing, but being. How many people cried at his funeral who were not members of CL![4] Enzo was a meeting point for everyone: patients, teachers, common folk, Americans, French, English, and who knows how many others. He had total dedication, as Father Giussani said, not just in the sense of commitment, but as a mentality and a way of understanding.

---

1. Born in Desio in 1922, Luigi Giussani (sometimes affectionately referred to as "don Giuss") studied theology at the Seminary of Venegono, where he was ordained a priest. Beginning in 1954 he taught religion in high schools and from 1964 to 1990 he taught Introduction to Theology at the Catholic University of Milan. Starting in the mid-fifties, he gave birth to and led the ecclesial Movement of education to the faith that would take the name Communion and Liberation, now present in Italy and in eighty countries around the world. He is the author of numerous essays and books, including *The Religious Sense, The Risk of Education, Why the Church?, The Origin of the Christian Claim, In Search of the Human Face, L'io, il potere, le opere*, and *Is It Possible to Live This Way?* Luigi Giussani died in Milan on February 22, 2005.

2. Communion and Liberation is the ecclesial Movement of education in the faith brought forth by the charism of Father Luigi Giussani which is now present in eighty countries worldwide. On February 11, 1982, the Fraternity of Communion and Liberation (the adult version of the Movement) was recognized by the Holy See as an Association of the Faithful of Pontifical Right.

3. *Traces* is a monthly publication of Communion and Liberation, available in several languages.

4. "CL" stands for "Communion and Liberation."

"For Enzo," Giancarlo goes on, "friendship was the point where destiny, that is, Christ, made Himself visible and became a point of comparison. He truly relied on friendship. God's designs are strange. Sometimes you think that what you need most is what gets taken away.

"The last time we met, just us two, was in the early spring of 1999. He had called to say, 'Let's get together and talk about ourselves, about life.' I said, 'Sure,' and so that he wouldn't have to come all the way from Bologna to Milan, I offered to meet him halfway. So Enzo and I made an appointment to meet at a restaurant in Piacenza that he knew, whose owner was one of his fans. We ate two local specialties and drank grappa. We talked about everything, from the university to work. We were together a couple of hours, then we both went our ways."

I go from Milan to Bologna, where Davide speaks of an "all-embracing friendship." "You couldn't live a moment or a fraction of your life without sharing it. Enzo provoked this reaction in the people he met, giving himself totally to the relationship with the other person. For us young college students, who saw an adult so involved with us, that relationship was becoming strikingly indispensable in the face of any other plausible attraction or duty. Everybody who met him has been changed, at least in his or her love for the Church and for Christ."

It was "life lived together" in the 1980's, and Davide remembers the first vacations in the mountains, the CLU équipes,[5] the public positions taken in the universities, Zanussi's film about Pope John Paul II, the defense of Solidarność, the expansion of this friendship to include more and more new friends. "Then there was also the fraternity, which used to change every year because it had never been lived with a deep enough level of decision."

In Modena, Cristina describes to me the friendship she lived with Enzo as the experience of a good "that transcends every limit and hardship, a good that endures despite every refusal and every doubt, a good that makes you daring in dealing with reality beyond every calculation and conquest."

Her encounter with Piccinini, which happened when Cristina was fifteen years old and had recently been drawn to CL in the community of *Gioventù Studentesca* (GS),[6] was the unexpected encounter with someone who embodied a humanity that was different from the usual, in that it was able to provoke the truest questions of the heart and to allow her to taste a correspondence she had never experienced before. Enzo had given her a ride in his car to take her to a meeting of GS students. That brief trip is fixed in her memory.

---

5. "CLU" stands for the Movement of Communion and Liberation at the university level; "équipes" are leadership meetings of CLU.

6. *Gioventù Studentesca* is the Movement of students which arose from the charism of Father Luigi Giussani during the years when he was teaching in high schools. Today, *Gioventù Studentesca* is the Movement of Communion and Liberation in its presence among high school students.

"His strong leadership, the barrage of the questions he asked, gave me the impression of a man who was energetic like few others, who knew what he was talking about, who didn't speak empty words, who constantly challenged you to enter the heart of the issue with him. In an instant my whole world as a teenager was turned upside down, and the partial answers I had put together for myself came crumbling down. So I found myself wondering, 'Who am I? What do I really know, not by hearsay, but by having experienced it myself? What do I really love?' This was Enzo's first impact on me, and so it remained to the end, getting deeper over time.

"I recall," continues Cristina, "some of the verses from the *Spoon River Anthology* by Edgar Lee Masters: *Yet all the while I hungered for meaning in my life. And now I know that we must lift the sail/ And catch the winds of destiny/ Wherever they drive my boat.* That's it, this need to lift the sail and let ourselves be pushed by Someone else, in an adventure of friendship, where we are not the ones holding the reins.

"Enzo loved us, which is why he challenged us about everything, even about our romantic relationships. '*Why do you want to go with that guy?*' 'Because I love him.' '*And what does he have to do with it?*' 'Well, he loves me too.' '*Yes, ok, but what does he have to do with it?*' It was not Twenty Questions, but a way for us to get to the bottom of the issues. Nobody had ever talked to us like that. We used to wonder, 'Where does a guy like this come from?' How did he know what reality is made of, how 'the smoke turns,' as he used to say, as if saying to us again and again, 'Wake up and smell the air!' He was driven by an ideal that resulted in questions that would not let you escape: 'Who do you answer to for the things you do? Who did you answer to when you got out of bed this morning?' Woe to you if you answered, 'To myself'!"

The GS kids of the community of Modena were (to use their words) "scared" but at the same time "fascinated" by Enzo's presence and by the way he "handed his life over" to them. "What he said was not just words, not just a wordy disquisition about the truth. Even before answering, you were already doing things for the community, giving everything for your friends. In an instant, the Ideal resulted, for example, in a demand for strict punctuality in meetings, because *in our midst is a God that we answer to*, so that those who came late ended up being sent back home."

For those who lived through that period of GS in Modena under Piccinini's guidance in the late seventies, it is impossible to forget "riding your bicycle, even during the night, to reach the place where we were meeting, because Enzo used to call us together at any time, and his invitations, even for seemingly trivial reasons, always had an air of solemnity that only he could give. Or we went hundreds of miles to find something beautiful, wherever it was, or to taste new foods in places only Enzo knew. It was a passion for life, which was changing the rhythm of our days, which was making us, sixteen and seventeen-year-old kids, as responsible as adults, which was creating a complete belonging to the unity we shared. And in the midst of all this flurry, maybe as Enzo was riding alongside you on your way home, an unexpected question would suddenly pop out: *So are you willing to give your life to Christ?* This is how eternity was bursting into our young lives."

There is one last incident that seals those days in Cristina's memory and explains what friendship meant for Piccinini. "It was my senior year, 'the first serious test of life,' as he used to say. I was in my room in the attic, the refuge of my perennial worries. The doorbell rings. It was Enzo, unexpectedly come to see me, for no reason at all, in the middle of an ordinary afternoon."

Every June in the expanse of Martyrs' Square in Carpi, near Modena, there is a festival alive with games, cultural events, and testimonials. It is an event that has been going on since 1984 and that arose from one of Piccinini's insights. In an interview for the Enzo Piccinini Foundation's newsletter, Nadia recalls that moment, a Saturday afternoon, sitting on a bench, while many people were passing the time in Martyrs' Square. "At one point Enzo says, 'How will all these people meet Christ? How will they live without him? It's a shame that all these people couldn't meet Christ.'" From this question, the idea was born of having a festival and holding it in the square, in the heart of the city, so that everyone could join in. It was a completely new initiative, because up to that point the square was used only for public meetings sponsored by the city, and it was an imposing challenge for the small group of young people who back then made up the community of CL in Carpi. However, backed by Piccinini's enthusiasm, "we started to get a move on, and we had the festival, just three weeks later."

"For me," Nadia continues, "friendship with Enzo, even without realizing it, meant an encounter with Christ. It was the friendship of Christ. It was something so all-embracing that I probably would never have come back to the Church if it hadn't come to me in this form. Enzo was not an easy person to deal with; you often fought with him. He used to constantly challenge you and ask you, 'What are you alive for? What do you hope in? What do you rely on?' It was a daily friendship that that included everything. He'd come back from the hospital in the evening and he'd find time to come meet us almost every day. With him, you knew that the Movement was not parallel to life, but that it had to do with life; it was essential for living."

In his office in Milan, Giorgio talks to me about Piccinini, as a member of the group of friends who gathered around Father Luigi Giussani. What shone in Enzo was "a human loyalty that showed itself as loyalty in the questions he used to ask don Giuss about everything, even the most knotty questions, never diminishing his desire, as if desire could find an answer all by itself.

"Enzo's most important feature," says Giorgio, "was a passion for justice, as God's justice. That is, he wanted things to be as they should be. And this desire grew into a love for the person, understood as the realization of this justice. Only in this way can we understand his full relationship with thousands of people in many parts of Italy and abroad, as a desire that the destiny of these people be affirmed in life, in every detail, from their work to their growth as people, to the conditions of their families. His experience of faith was a complete response to the needs of people today.

"When Enzo would tell me about some friend who had problems," Giorgio continues, "I was always surprised by his ability to describe the situation in every detail, and to grasp with extraordinary sensitivity even the most delicate aspects. He, who was also a very busy surgeon, could take in every detail of the personalities of the friends he met, and remember them precisely. It is a clear indication of his refinement of spirit, a rare quality, which is the opposite of ideology. Refinement of spirit leads to the mystery. It is the capacity to identify with the person in affection for his destiny: thus it grasps even the details and fills you up with them. And then I also remember Enzo's laugh, full of wonder and joy—the laughter of someone who knows how to enjoy life."

Padua is also on my journey in Enzo's footsteps. Ca' Edimar is in the far northwest outskirts of the city. It is a place that welcomes young people in difficulty and accompanies them on a path of education for work. The meeting hall is dedicated to Piccinini, who was among the first to grasp the full importance of this charitable work and to appreciate its value, prodding his friends to help it grow. Mario, Ca' Edimar's founder, tells me how his friendship with Enzo grew. Both took part in the Movement's National Council, but at first there was a certain distance between them owing somewhat to mutual respect. Then came a phone call.

"His 'thank you' at the end of our conversation blew that distance out of the water. I realized that, in an instant, he had cleared away all the preconceptions. That's what he was like: if he thought a relationship was true, he was ready to risk everything on it, without being influenced by any past grievances or misunderstandings. He took no offense over difficulties. I remember a long and lively debate on the education situation in our country. He attacked hard, as was his character, but when I spoke to him about the idea of a new artistic school he immediately got enthused. We ended up thinking about how we could make it happen. Here, too, we had started far apart, but then, faced with the possibility of something good, Enzo showed his greatness in recognizing it and jumping on it."

One of the incidents recalled by Mario concerns his son Daniele, who had decided to pursue a career as a musician. "Enzo came to Padua for a conference, and afterwards I went to greet him with my son, who was going to perform his first concert in two days. Daniele talked to him about why he had chosen music. Piccinini immediately affirmed his passion by giving him an assignment. He said, 'When I was young I also had a punk band and I played guitar. You will have to work in a harsh, even degrading environment. But it's there that you have a great task, to bring yourself and what you believe in to that place. So remember to stay connected to real friends.' That conversation marked a turning point in my son's life. Two days later Enzo called me. I thought, 'What could have happened?' But he only wanted to know how Daniele's concert had gone."

In January 1998, during the traditional evening festivities on the eve of Epiphany, a dramatic incident occurred in Padua. While the families of the Fraternity of Communion and Liberation of Padua, including many children, were gathered around a bonfire, there was an explosion. Fifty people were injured and two of them, Massimo and Giulia, died from the serious injuries they sustained. Some of those recuperating in the hospital were in intensive care. Informed of the incident, Father Luigi Giussani called Enzo the next morning and asked him to go immediately to Padua to be near his friends: "Help them as much as you can."

"In the most critical period," says Giampaolo, "as soon as he finished his daily work as a surgeon, Enzo got in his car and drove to Padua. I often went along with him. In the hospital, he took stock of the situation with the intensive care staff. Then he went to the homes of the families of the most seriously wounded to give them news and to visit those who had been discharged. For all these people Piccinini had become a reference point to look to for comfort in that tragedy. Every day back and forth, from Bologna to Padua, to go and see, visit, talk, support and stay close to the patients and their families."

The chances of recovery for some of the most seriously injured were very slim. Enzo, as an experienced surgeon, helped to recognize the damage done and to choose the course of action. He stood alongside his colleagues from Padua, sparing no effort in the attempt to save his friends.

Graziano, regional responsible[7] for the Fraternity of Communion and Liberation in the Veneto region, tells me how the budding relationship with Enzo solidified through those painful days. "This friendship," Graziano explains, "was not something I chose. At first, in fact, I wasn't even enthusiastic about it. It was clearly proposed; it was given to me by Father Luigi Giussani."

About a year before the dramatic events of 1998, Piccinini had become the visitor[8] of the Veneto region and of the whole Adriatic coast as far as Puglia. "Enzo came to us," continues Graziano, "at a time when our relationship was marked by differences of opinion and by prejudice. Father Giussani called me and said, 'Welcome Enzo as you welcome me; accept him as a friend as you are friends with me.' Now with don Giuss I had the freedom of full confidence and friendship. I used to tell him everything, as a father you open your heart to, about beautiful things and hard things. And so I felt like his request was outrageous. So I said, 'It's impossible.' But Father Giussani answered, 'Since Enzo is someone who is completely one with my heart, I am asking you to make friends with him.'

---

7. "Responsible" is a term roughly equivalent to "leader," used in Communion and Liberation for those who help guide groups of the Movement.

8. A "visitor" is a person directly appointed by the one ultimately responsible for Communion and Liberation, and has the task of befriending and following the life of the CL communities in a given area of Italy or abroad, pointing out the direction of the path in accord with the charism of Father Luigi Giussani.

"At first I resisted, but then by the grace of God I did the only good thing I could do. I obeyed, and I started to treat Enzo as a friend—not out of fondness, but because Giussani had asked me to. Beginning with this act of obedience, what happened in '98 was the soil that an extraordinary friendship with Enzo grew out of and blossomed, a friendship so intense that I could never have imagined it. We usually think that our real friends are the ones we pick, but real friends are those who are given to us by the Lord so that we can walk toward Him. This is how I came to realize how true Father Giussani's words are, who says that friendship and obedience are part of the same human stock, that they're the same thing. There is no such thing as friendship without obedience."

The dramatic incident when the huge Epiphany bonfire turned itself into a bomb through a series of unforeseeable circumstances took place in Padua on January 5, 1998 at nine in the evening. It was a very foggy night. Enzo was already in town the next morning at ten. One by one, he visited all the people who had been wounded, then in tears called Father Giussani who had this message sent out:

> To all the fraternity groups in Italy: In the fraternity of Padua, the Lord is saying something to all of us. As a first response to hearing to the tragic news that has impacted the entire fraternity of Padua, as mysterious as the mysterious death of Jesus, we first of all ask the Lord, through the intercession of the Blessed Mother, to help our friends in Veneto. The mysterious purpose in this tragedy, to the degree that we can understand God's ways of dealing with mankind, is a call to conversion for us, that each of us may give his contribution in his lifetime to the glory of Christ, crucified and risen. Let us all live the pain of this moment together in this way.

On the feast of Epiphany, Father Giussani's words were read to the friends of the Fraternity of CL who were gathered in prayer in the chapel of the hospital in Padua. "Up to that moment," continues Graziano, "despair was rampant among us and it seemed as if it was all over, given the scale of the disaster, so full of potential harm and negative consequences. Then that message, coming first of all as a simple relief and as the closeness of a father, and also as a judgment that took in all the things that were happening in such a dizzying and painful way, marked a turning point. From that point on Father Giussani took us by the hand. He called every day to keep us company in our suffering. One part of his hand was Enzo, who lived those days among us with a striking attention to every one of the people involved. Piccinini was also a great surgeon, and he directed all his skills toward a proper assessment of the problems of his injured friends and a rapid identification of the most effective treatments. Enzo especially accompanied us in defining the question that this tragedy posed: What really held our lives together? Where had we placed our hope?"

Of all the people injured, Gino's situation appeared particularly critical; he had acute breathing problems and severe chest trauma. After falling into a coma he had been operated on, but infection set in. "One day Enzo told me that, from the clinical point of view, there was nothing left to do, and that our wounded friend probably had only a few hours to live. I called Father Giussani to tell him what was happening, but don Giuss said, 'I prayed on my knees to the Lord for all of you and for Gino. Do not worry about him; he will get better. It's not Gino's life that the Lord is asking for, but for your conversion, that your hearts become bigger and truer, more able to love Jesus.' Along with Enzo and Cinzia, Gino's wife, we kept these words alive in our hearts for months. Gino stayed in the hospital a long time. Every day the medical reports spelled out the dramatic seriousness of the situation, but we prayed and waited for the fulfillment of the promise that Father Giussani had made. Finally, in July, Gino came back home, and it was a great joy for us. So we became friends with Enzo, looking at what the Lord was doing in our midst, even in our suffering.

"This was '98: sometimes, as Father Giussani said, 'The Lord comes into our house like a hurricane comes to Florida.' Through our great friend Enzo, Father Giussani's goodness came to us and everything that from a human point of view seemed destroyed was slowly rebuilt.

"A year later, on Holy Saturday in 1999, Father Giussani invited me to lunch with Gino. At that engagement we also met Enzo and his family," Graziano concludes. "It was the last time I saw Piccinini. Father Giussani told us, 'You are here together, and you become friends because I asked you to and this is something great.' We usually think that friendship is a thing that belongs to us. But friendship is the best of all things because it is given by Someone else."

His Excellency Luigi Negri, bishop of San Marino Montefeltro, also links Enzo's memory to the word friendship. "He was a man of strong, passionate, all-embracing friendship, the sort of friendship that could even seem too much, but which then showed itself to be tender and very human. He was above all a friend to the friends that the Lord had given him, to whom He bound him by virtue of the exquisite and entirely Giussanian notion of preference. This preference, however, expanded, so to speak, to the whole community, so that even those most on the fringes felt involved in his friendship. But then—and this is the thing that touched me most about him when I heard him speak or saw him living—this friendship became love for the Church and a passion for every person that Providence put in his path, beginning with his patients. He was a man of friendship and mission. This is the holiness of the people of God.

Chapter Two
The Encounter

"I am an atheist, who became a Christian *by chance*," Enzo used to say of himself, "because I come from the place where atheism was born, the low plains of Emilia. I grew up breathing in the pragmatism which is typical of Emilia, where you have to do, do, do. For them, metaphysics is nothing more than the opinion of a sick mind. This was the sort of climate I grew up in. So for me, Christianity has been a real adventure. It was like a gamble and, if I am part of Christianity, it's because there's a challenge inside it. The challenge is that Christianity does not mean that a man becomes a little bit less than others, because he has some extra moral obligations; it means real humanity."

Bagno is the district in "the low plains of Emilia" where Enzo, born June 5, 1951, spent the first years of his life. It's just a handful of houses near Rubiera, in the province of Reggio Emilia. There were fourteen in the family, "all provided for by the hard work of farmers, which was done mostly by hand back then," says his mother Ilde. Living with him in the big farmhouse were his grandparents, his parents, five brothers, his aunt Maria, and another uncle who was married with one son. His father was president of Catholic Action.

"In the evening when the bells would ring, Enzo, who was only three years old at the time, would tell me, 'Mamma, it's time to say prayers.'"

During the summer vacation of 1965, on the feast of Saints Peter and Paul, Enzo, then fourteen years old, took his bicycle to go to Holy Mass. Pedaling in front of him, "Indian file," was his brother Sergio, three years younger. They were riding on one of those narrow roads in the low plains that run along the banks of the ditches. A passing truck struck them. Enzo came back home alone, screaming, "Mamma, they've killed Sergio." "It was the hardest moment of his childhood," continues Ilde. "He wandered through the fields alone and wouldn't talk with anyone. At night he'd come down from his room and say, 'Mamma, I can't sleep.' I would answer him, 'We have to accept it.'"

Enzo "wanted to study," she says, but keeping a child in school was not easy for a large farming family. Help came in the form of the friendship of Father Girolamo, a Servite priest. So Enzo was able to continue his studies in private schools. His early middle school years were spent at Monte Fano, near Macerata; he did his first high school years in a classical lyceum in Bologna, and his later high school years in Ancona, as the host of an institute of the Servants of Mary, but he attended the Rinaldini public school, where he obtained his diploma in classical education in 1970.

Enzo and Fiorisa met at the Rinaldini high school in Ancona, on the school benches. "It was 1968," recalls Fiorisa, "and partly out of temperament, partly out of coercion from my parents, partly out of an innate bourgeois mentality, I kept myself at a good distance from the spirited discussions on social and political issues that used to captivate kids back then." Enzo's first approach was of the cultural sort. "He offered me a book to read called *The Mill on the Floss*, by an English author I had never heard of before."

This gesture struck Fiorisa, who says, "At that time I was looking for a real human relationship, a meaningful one, but I didn't know how to express this need to anyone. I tended to daydream instead, to isolate. I had no friends except at school, but I more or less found all my classmates to be shallow, uncaring and—why not?—even a little bit ignorant. Enzo was different. He was full of life, and certainly more cultivated than all the others. His expressions and sayings in the dialect of Reggiano kept us laughing. The class nicknamed him Super Enzo, or the Czechoslovakian, because of his blond Nordic looks. I became Super Fiorisa, because I was interested in him and I was one of the top students. Our two personalities complemented one another, and our affection deepened.

"The teachers had a love/hate relationship with Enzo. Thanks to his comments and his critical spirit, our classes were more interesting, even if they thought he was disrespectful," a fact that earned him a bad grade in conduct and a negative report by Father Bruno of the Servants of Mary about his "unwillingness to study." Meanwhile, his passion for sports grew: basketball, volleyball, and especially soccer, which kept him involved in local summer tournaments and in hard workouts.

Enzo's return home at the end of high school brought with it a "complete rebellion against the issue of Christianity" and the refusal to take part in certain formalities. It was at that time that he began his militant activism in a far left group, which was based on the ideological foundations of 1968 and was beginning to theorize about the possibility of armed struggle. The group, composed of young militants coming from the ranks of the Italian Communist Party, was called the Chamber[1] and was based in Reggio Emilia. To the fascination of Enzo, who carried in his heart "a need for basic justice" and the desire to commit himself to working for societal change, the organization demanded total adherence and a commitment to militancy. "It was a heavy experience," recalled Enzo, "because I came out of it when they went into hiding."

The far left's militant activism was opposed by his family. "One day," recalls his mother Ilde, "one of his companions came to our house who later be-

---

1. In Italian, the Appartamento.

came one of the Red Brigades. They went up to his room to talk. When he left, I told Enzo I didn't want to see this in our house ever again."

But it was not family opposition that distanced Enzo from that "maddened militancy," from that "iron organization," but an encounter.

Members of the Chamber "used to organize seminars on Marx that lasted hours and hours." Taking part in these study sessions were also three young men from One Way, a Catholic student organization founded in Reggio Emilia that was connected to the Milanese *Gioventù Studentesca* movement. Enzo, struck by the way those three stayed together, began to grow interested in them. Out of this was born a curiosity to "go and see what they were doing."

"They used to meet every day," recalled Enzo, "in the crypt of the cathedral of Reggio Emilia for evening prayer, with the recitation of the Psalms. I wanted to participate too, but since they knew that I belonged to the Chamber, they were afraid. So they used to send someone to talk with me while they were praying the Psalms, and I was always left outside. When I figured out their game I said, 'Look, I don't want to do anything wrong. I just want to get to know you. Take me with you once.' So I finally participated in the Psalms. It seemed like a dream come true to me, even if I didn't understand a thing."

The leaders of the Chamber realized that something was changing in Enzo. They started to doubt his position and they investigated. "You met those new guys? What do you think of them?" One of the captains of the Chamber went along with Enzo to Piazza San Prospero before the recitation of the Psalms. A decisive conversation took place on that occasion. This is how Enzo remembered it: "The captain who had come with me put his arm around me and started to tell me, 'See, they're good guys, but they have a one-track mind. Everything's about Jesus Christ, in every possible way.' He was saying these things as if he were talking about a serious handicap.

"Every other time when religious topics were brought up, I always used to fire back instinctively with a preconceived hatred. This time, however, I didn't react. So the Chamber realized that I was no longer entirely their property. For the first time, the word 'Jesus Christ' no longer referred to a moral law or to something that had to be done, but to a group of friends that I liked. In fact, even without knowing it, I had already made a choice."

Enzo's experience of Christianity began in a new way with the encounter with a group of people who "were living a friendship I had never seen before, but had always wanted."

Fiorisa noticed that something new had happened in Enzo's life. "After his encounter with these new friends, I realized that something had changed in him. Before then, he was very critical of his parents and of Christianity. He was put off by purely formal religiosity which had no attractive power." Afterwards, however, "he used to make me read books and articles about the experience of Christianity that I sometimes could not understand." About himself, Enzo wrote, "What I'm frantically looking for is nothing but authentic Christianity, and in the Movement this is the proposal that matters most."

Once high school was over, his relationship with Fiorisa passed through a period that she remembers as "overwhelming nostalgia" because of the distance between them. "I've made up my mind to never forget you," Enzo wrote at the time. "I've told you over and over. I feel like my heart and my whole being is deeply bound to you forever. Ahead of us, I know, lies a long road. I have to finish that road as an adult; that is, I need to become a man, so I can offer you my life with complete awareness, and a bond that will last into eternity. Do not forget me. Live your days in peace and think, if you wish, that next to you, from this day on, there is someone who loves you, a heart that beats in time with yours."

That same summer of 1970, Enzo enrolled in the College of Medicine and Surgery at the University of Modena. "We tried to help in every way," recalls his mother Ilde, "and to help pay for his studies, I raised and sold rabbits and chickens. Enzo also made many sacrifices, and our family doctor gave us a hand by lending him his books so he could prepare for exams. His classmates were spoiled rich kids. But he was the son of farmers. In Modena, Enzo stayed in an apartment with some friends from the CL Movement. He'd leave on Monday and come back Friday night."

Fiorisa, on the other hand, enrolled in the College of Biology at the University of Bologna. "When my girlfriend was in Bologna," says Enzo, "I used to always go to see her on my scooter. I had a big one with two seats that could barely move. So I used to slipstream trucks to take advantage of the lower air pressure, and so was able to increase my speed a little. But when I got there I was all black! If anyone else had made me do it for any other reason, I would have beaten him. But I would do it and I didn't even notice, in fact, I was really glad because that woman's face came along with me even in the midst of difficulty. When you focus too much on the difficulty, it means that your ideal has gone to hell! It's the ideal that lights up the path of life, like that woman's face did. I had no problem following those trucks; I would have hung on to the tailpipe. The problem is remembering that the ideal is present and comes along with us. Then you can offer up your difficulty, too."

His relationship with the young people in the Movement of Communion and Liberation, which was beginning to take its first steps at the University of Modena and elsewhere, was not an easy thing for Enzo, partly due to his temperament, which he himself used to describe as "self-centered, prone to anger, all-consuming, with an energy that even I don't know where it comes from."

"People in CL," Enzo recounted, "would sometimes come to see me and I would tell them to go to hell." However, their insistent pleas for him to come to an assembly at the University and to speak on behalf of the Movement of Communion and Liberation provoked an unexpected change. After refusing more than a few times, Enzo accepted the invitation and prepared the text of a speech with the help of his friends.

When the time came for a representative of CL to speak in the assembly hall, crammed with people, where the leaders of other student movements had spoken before, there was "total silence." However, the speech he had written out wasn't at all good enough for Enzo, so he folded it up, put it in his pocket, and improvised on the spot a critical judgment on the situation of the university and on the protests that were taking place. He concluded with these words: "I am here to say that all these things do not fulfill your life. For me, life has changed because I encountered a reality that is called Jesus Christ." At first there were loud whispers in the hall, then laughter broke out. So Enzo went back to the microphone and shouted, "I dare any one of you to come outside and say the same thing."

This was how the bond between Enzo and his friends in Communion and Liberation at University of Modena was solidified. "I found myself again," he disclosed, "because almost by instinct I relived the encounter I had had, thanks to those relationships that would almost bug the heck out of me. I had left because of a sentimental and ultimately moralistic judgment. I came back because Christianity isn't something to be simply understood, but an experience to be embraced just as it is."

After that assembly, Enzo began to participate more and more deeply in the life of Communion and Liberation in Modena, and in 1972 he became the driving force behind an intense social activity project on the city's east side. Some programs witnessed an outstanding level of participation from the local populace, especially from many young people.

In 1973 Enzo and Fiorisa were married. On July 1 of that year, Enzo wrote, "Lord, I thank you because my path is clear. I beg you to give me the strength and the will for this marriage to not be a private matter as the world wants it to be, but the place where we will call one another back to life for Christ and for his Church. The sacramental nature of marriage makes us adults in the faith. The adult is aware that salvation, that is, this new way of life, is not just for his own satisfaction or that of a few, but is God's plan for the world. Thus the Christian sees himself as a sign of the Christian community and as a factor of the whole world. He learns to love and to act on his faith in every situation, that is, to desire that communion may grow in every environment, that places where Christianity is experienced may increase, where life can find its meaning, which is Christ who died and rose again."

Starting in those years, the development of Enzo's personal relationship with Father Luigi Giussani was at the center of his path of conversion. Enzo described how that friendship was born, that relationship of fatherhood and sonship that would mark a turning point in his life: "When I first met Giussani he took me into his heart. I don't know why. It's inexplicable. He had others who were much more prepared than I was and who were more influential in living Christianity. Yet from that day on, he always kept track of me, at first out of the corner of his eye, and then more and more intensely. At first, knowing that if he tried to teach me the catechism, I wouldn't have stayed with him more than two minutes, he gave me novels to read. They were novels that had struck him. I would read these books and then he would ask me what I thought about them."

The first novel that Father Luigi Giussani gave Enzo to read was *To Every Man a Penny* by the English writer Bruce Marshall. To Enzo, the book seemed to be "the usual stuff of priests," too full of religious matters. He read only a few pages, then closed the book and set it aside. When about a month later he met Father Luigi Giussani again, he heard him asking what he had thought about the novel.

"I made an immediate connection," Enzo continued. "He's a priest; I have to say something that priests would like. So I acted serious and I answered, 'I would have to say that it taught me to pray.' Giussani started laughing, and I realized that it was useless to cheat with him. Then he said, 'Listen, Enzo, this is a book that you read on the beach.' A skeleton to keep in the closet. That's how the story began."

In 1975 Enzo took on the responsibility for the Movement of Communion and Liberation in Modena that at the time was mainly composed of young people—students in GS, college students, some young workers, and a few young families.

One of the youngest members was Luigi, who had met the Movement of CL at the age of only eleven during summer vacation, taking part in recreational activities put on at Holy Family parish by a group of CL youth in September. His parents were not in favor of his participation in GS, but the friendship had remained through middle school and high school. Luigi remembers that "Enzo had a very charismatic personality which held me in awe, a tough character, but I realized that he loved me and I was fascinated by his personality.

"Everything in the community of Modena revolved around him, beginning with the experience of *Gioventù Studentesca*. If something was happening, if there was trouble at school, the first question was, 'Have you talked with Enzo?' He was the point of comparison and you understood, from his natural authority, that it was essential, in any circumstance, to talk it over with him. He would always try to wake us up. He would prod us and help us. I used to talk about everything with him, little things and big things.

"When one of our friends, a great guy who had just started college, died in a car accident, Enzo took us by the hand and helped us discover that behind this death there was a mystery that could be embraced. He did it through concrete gestures. For example, he taught us to be close to our friend's parents, with care and extraordinary tenderness. Outside the church after the funeral rites, he told us, 'Now you have to grow up.' I realized in that moment that the purpose of the Movement is to make our humanity blossom. He was the prototype of this greatness."

With the GS kids, Enzo would use the same method that he had learned from Giussani, and he would propose meaningful books for them to read. "Once," Luigi remembers, "he made us read Joseph Roth's story *The Legend of the Holy Drinker*, then asked for our opinion. I said that I hadn't liked it at all and when he asked why, I said that reality is not like this and that the protagonist is just a poor unlucky individual. Enzo got very angry and told me that I'd understood nothing of the text and the meaning of grace. And it was true because for me, having grown up with the mindset that you're worthwhile only if you're productive, the concept of grace was totally unknown. Now, every so often I go back and reread that story that opened a new dimension in my life."

During his high school years, Luigi had become the GS responsible alongside Enzo; however, his belonging to the Movement of Communion and Liberation was long hampered by his parents. There is an episode in this story that explains the greatness of Enzo's fatherhood toward the kids in the community. "So that I could take part in common activities and see my friends, I would sometimes escape from home," Luigi continues. "I did it once during a summer vacation in the mountains. I put pillows under my blankets so my parents wouldn't realize I was gone, and ran out at night to catch the train. I was sixteen years old then, and the next morning when I got to the hotel where the GS meeting was in progress, Enzo asked me what I was doing there. I answered, 'I escaped.' He told me, 'You have to go back home.' After informing them where I was, he made me go back to my parents. A few days later there was an assembly of the communities in Modena, and I spoke up, explaining why I was happy to belong to the Movement. Enzo, who was leading the event, came down from the stage and hugged me. I felt Enzo's fatherhood more than ever and I will never forget that embrace. It was the embrace of a man who loved me and I wanted nothing more than to be loved like that. Nothing mattered more than that."

Meanwhile, the Piccinini family was growing. After Chiara was born, Maria, Pietro and Anna Rita came along. Father Luigi Giussani travelled to Modena to baptize the two youngest. Along with the children, financial difficulties also grew because Enzo, after getting a degree in medicine in 1976, had started a specialization in general surgery and his specialization scholarship was not enough to meet all the family's needs. For this reason his mother Ilde continued to help him.

In 1979, his eldest daughter Chiara was about to begin elementary school. Aware of the importance of an educational proposal consistent with the ideals being lived in the family, Enzo suggested to some friends who also had young children, starting a school in Modena run by a cooperative of parents and teachers.

On May 2, 1979, The Caravan[2] was formed. Enzo was the first director of this educational operation. He laid out its framework and guided its basic decisions.

Fiorisa recounts that at the beginning "there were three or four children, including our daughter Chiara." The premises where the school first had its start had been provided by a religious institute run by nuns on the outskirts of Modena. Back then The Caravan was tiny, a seed destined to grow. "There were only two teachers, one for kindergarten and one for elementary school in a combined class, first, second, and third grades all together." Enzo himself would

---

2. In Italian, "La Carovana."

lead training sessions with the teachers and with their other friends in the cooperative, engaged in various ways in the organization of The Caravan. He would also invite the parents and would ask them not to simply delegate the path of their children's education to the school, but to be involved themselves. Their reference book was *The Risk of Education* by Father Luigi Giussani, and there were constant references to the passion for the human heart that their great friend and teacher had.

It was from him that Enzo had learned a new way to look at children. "The way to love them, to use an image that shows the depth of the question, is that when you have them in your arms, you're holding them to you, you're feeling that tenderness that makes you melt, it's at that moment that you should step back and look at them, wondering, 'What will become of them?' This is how to really love them, because they have a destiny. They are not yours; they have their freedom, which is their belonging to the Mystery. What will become of them? This is the true position, love for their destiny, a basic judgment that binds them to you forever and creates a new relationship, a different kind of concern for others and their freedom."

In those same years when the school was coming into being, Enzo, with the help of a group of friends, became the director of Poetry Hill,[3] a cultural center in Modena. The activities of this association are still a reference point for many people in Modena.

His increasing work commitments, his travels abroad for his specialization as a surgeon, and his dedication to the Movement would leave Enzo very little time that he could devote to his family. "Of course there were difficulties," says Fiorisa. "Maybe we needed to make an important decision and he wasn't there. But I knew that everything would be come out all right, even if it took patience. I tried to explain this to our children and to help them understand that their father's commitments and his absence were a plus for our lives. And Enzo would always make sure that we were surrounded by friends who shared the journey."

His daughter Maria remembers that "when I was little, the relationship I had with my father was a little bit love and hate. I would cry and cry over his absence and I would always pray to God to have him come back quickly. In fact, when he was not home our family was out of whack, so to speak. But when he was home, there was real joy. He would shake up our usual way of being together and challenge it, and he would help us get to the bottom of what we were living: school, current events, feelings. He would not leave us in peace, but ultimately that was what we were hoping for, and he kept us together."

"True, he was often gone, but I always felt his strong presence in my daily life as a foundational authority," adds Anna Rita. "I felt his presence especially in the unity that we had with our mom, like he was completely present inside our relationship with her. Likewise in school, at The Caravan, because everyone who was close to me and everyone who taught me was a friend of Dad. Besides,

---

3. In Italian, "La collina della poesia."

I had learned to accept his very absence as an embrace, because what he was involved in was for our good; it was an opportunity for our growth as well.

"I was really glad when he would come home, because I would see how much he adored us. I remember our Sunday dinners when we were all together as amazing occasions because he would never waste a minute, but would talk through all the aspects of our lives with us. Over the years I saw his attitude toward us changing. We were a father and his children, but we had grown to be friends, sharing a deep friendship."

Piccinini used to describe the outcome of this way of being together by recalling one of those Sunday dinners when the family was gathered, when he addressed this question to his children, who as they were growing up had entered the community of Communion and Liberation: "Why do you belong to CL? There is a reason why I'm asking you: I realized that in all these years I have never talked to you about the Movement; I have never explained to you what it is." His children's answer pointed out two clear reasons: "Look, Dad, first of all, the intensity of your dedication to the CL community has always struck, fascinated, or in any case raised questions for us. Secondly, whenever your friends would come to our house we saw a friendship among you that we liked, and that we felt must be true for us, too."

Summer vacations were very intense for Enzo's family: "You were never idle; there was a positive connection in everything, even in resting. There was always a purpose," continues Anna Rita. "Maybe we would all get up at seven in the morning because we had to walk to a cove where the sea was more beautiful, or we would all stay on the beach under the sun without swimming until we had finished a game that we had started together. Even during vacations his relationships with his friends never came to a standstill. There was always someone trying to reach him by phone, and we ourselves would choose where we went on vacation in order to be close to some community and to families that Dad had met."

After obtaining his degree in medicine, Enzo followed a specialization in surgery, studying with the teacher he most admired, Professor Angelo Conti. In 1980 Conti transferred to the University of Bologna and Enzo, who had in the meantime also obtained a specialization in vascular surgery, went along with him, staying beside him in university work. However, he maintained his residence and a concentrated network of relationships and activities in Modena.

Chapter Three
A Father, Because He Was a Son

In 1980 Enzo followed the direction of Giancarlo Cesana, which had been approved and supported by Father Luigi Giussani, and decisively took on the responsibility for the CL university students in Bologna, making a new group of young friends.

"With him as responsible, the community was led by a relentless, extremely energetic friendship, in accord with Piccinini's temperament and drive, so highly valued by Giussani," writes Massimo Camisasca in his book *Comunione e Liberazione. Il riconoscimento* [Communion and Liberation: The Recognition].[1]

Giancarlo clearly remembers the difficult steps which led to that choice. He had met Piccinini some years earlier, and had had the impression of "a cool cat, entirely absorbed by the one thousand activities of the Reggio Emilia community. And there really were a thousand."

Later on, in the late seventies, Giancarlo, out of all the national responsibles for Communion and Liberation in the universities, had been sent to Bologna, where there was one of the largest CLU communities, to support his friends. They were actually "a little blocked" by a certain "intellectualistic tendency" and by "an inferiority complex toward the Marxist ideology that was prevalent in those years in the institutions of higher learning."

But in the Bologna community, Giancarlo did not have a large following. So, remembering that "cool cat" from Reggio Emilia who was living in Modena and had transferred to Bologna for his work, he tracked him down and invited him to join the group of CLU responsibles.

Before accepting the invitation, Enzo "put up a little resistance." Some university students, including some members of CL, had just put out a flyer against him because in the first session of his exams he had flunked many students. Enzo's entry as a faculty member in the College of Medicine at the Uni-

---

1. Massimo Camisasca, *Comunione e Liberazione. Il riconoscimento* (Milan: San Paolo, 2006) 69–70.

versity of Bologna was thus greeted with a flyer which criticized him because he "was seen as too harsh in his judgments." Piccinini was certainly not intimidated and, with his fiery character, he publicly and strongly explained his reasons, attacking the authors of the critique. In any case, Enzo decided to accept the invitation and joined the responsibles.

"A deep sympathy between me and him immediately began to grow," Giancarlo continues, remembering the CLU diakonias[2] in Bologna as "rather cold." "Enzo always used to sit in the back. Eventually I asked him to speak up. I valued what he had to say and I would conclude the meeting without further comment. After the meeting we would leave together, walking to farthest bar on Strada Maggiore to get a drink and to talk about ourselves, and then we would go our ways, I to Milan and he to Modena. Enzo had a Peugeot diesel, the cheapest kind with the smallest engine, which already had thousands of miles on it and which Enzo would put thousands more on in the days to come."

Giancarlo involved Enzo more and more in CLU, to the point of suggesting to Father Giussani that he appoint Enzo as the ultimate responsible for the entire community of Bologna.

Alberto, a university student in Bologna who would later become part of the group of new responsibles working around Piccinini, recalls having been struck in his first encounters with Enzo by one of the aspects of his character: "His impetuous and sanguine temperament—his absolute insistence on entering into reality, with no wavering or hesitation. He was someone who really knew what his path was. Partly because of this, at the beginning, conversation with him was not simple. He would give very little room for discussion about anything that wasn't about lived experience. Only later did I realize that his discovery of the faith in his encounter with Father Giussani was his one and only weapon and resource, his one source of certainty. The encounter he had had determined the whole drama of his life and his relationships."

The first months of guiding CLU in Bologna were a sort of "interim period" for Enzo, as he got to know his new friends. Then in the summer of 1981 there was an event that marked a turning point. In August, Piccinini led the youth on a vacation in the mountains, in Santa Caterina Valfurva.

"One evening, during that vacation," says Alberto, "a fiery debate broke out, starting from an incident that had happened in the group from the College of Letters. One of our fellow students had had a stroke that had affected her memory centers. Some of our friends had stood by her side to help her along the difficult path of recovery and to regain her ability to read and write. As we talked about this incident, one of us said that, faced with such a person, our way of saying Christ had to be different from how we would speak his name to our other fellow students.

---

2. In the language of Communion and Liberation, a "diakonia" is a meeting of the leadership, that is, of the responsibles.

"Enzo suddenly interrupted us, saying, 'No, that's not it. Christ is true for everyone. Our problem is not how to speak his name, but to speak it.' The discussion went on at length and became the unifying theme of the following nights. Enzo would never let up; he would never give room for an emotional or sentimental understanding of our friendship."

The outcome of those days spent living together in the mountains was challenging. "Some guys left there demoralized and convinced that when it came to Enzo it was almost impossible to be understood." So "let him do it himself." They talked it over with Father Giancarlo, and he gave them this advice: "Try to see if Enzo might not be right." The students came back from their vacation in the mountains with this provocative suggestion.

The incident that Alberto recounts happened in August, and it seemed to put a rift between Enzo and some of those responsible for CLU in Bologna. In September, however, an unexpected phone call came from Piccinini's secretary. Some of the students who had been on the vacation in the mountains were being invited to supper. At table, Enzo said, "I'd like to become friends with you. If you're interested, we could all meet once a week and have something to eat together."

From that point a common journey began. "Enzo's invitation after that vacation was the last thing I expected," continues Alberto. "I was convinced that he would not give us a chance. But I was wrong. That was how a friendship was born that, along with the encounter I later lived with Father Giussani, was decisive for my life in terms of vocation, of work and of growing deeper in the faith. At that time, we met with Enzo every Monday in a restaurant in Bologna at Porta San Vitale. The theme of our meetings there was not how to organize the CLU, how to manage it or what activities to have, but our lives. He put his whole self into his relationship with us. That was how I discovered a way of living the Movement that I'd never seen before, with a familiarity that I can identify without hesitation as a true fatherhood. I used to confide in him about my concerns, my problems, my successes, my hardships. The same kind of trust came from him."

"In Bologna, Enzo devoted himself to the university students of the CL community with a great passion for education," Giancarlo confirms. "His aim was to help them grow, to bring out their personalities. From this point of view he was a true educator. Like all great educators, he was also a troublemaker. In every setting his presence was a challenge, that is, no one remained indifferent. He was always on the attack."

For Elena too, meeting Enzo in the early eighties is still unforgettable. "I was in my freshman year, and there was a meeting on the issue of abortion in the library of Saint Dominic. I had just come to Bologna, and I had gathered that the climate in CLU was very subdued. The guys would stay locked up in their apartments out of fear of the anarchists and the far leftists, after the threats and violence they had suffered in '77. I was coming from Rimini with an intense desire to live as a protagonist in college, but I found fear, disillusionment, and exhaustion."

However, during that meeting something new and unexpected occurred. At one point, Piccinini came forward from the back of the room and spoke with a tone that struck Elena: "He was decisive, certain, and full of enthusiasm." Enzo said on that occasion that if we do not know why it is worthwhile to live, it is pointless to get involved in the defense of life. We had forgotten the starting point.

Elena got to know Enzo better the following summer when, along with some friends, she was invited by Giancarlo to attend a national équipe of CLU. "I remember Enzo being always attached to Father Giussani and to the others from Milan. He always had something to say, and Father Giussani always kept him close by. And for his part, Piccinini would not let go of him for a moment."

Elena also remembers the vacation of the university students of Bologna at Santa Caterina Valfurva, recalling that it was marked by "constant battles." "During the day there were meetings, games, walks, songs, morning prayer. In the evening, until it was late, very late, we argued. Nothing that we had acquired was taken for granted. Enzo challenged everything and he pressed us with constant questions: 'Why? What does it mean? What do you really want? Why did you come on this vacation?' His presence shook up our lives, our choices, our friendship. No one could shrink from his challenging gaze." Then, one evening, that argument broke out, leaving some in tears, on the case of their friend with the stroke and how to talk to her about Jesus Christ.

"At the beginning of September I received an unexpected invitation to supper. Enzo didn't ask us to do something for the community, but to commit ourselves to the ideal, to the totality that our lives are called to. After we said yes that night, the next morning I received his first telephone call, composed of a single word: 'News?' He would always ask us this: 'News?' Even two hours after we had seen one another: 'News?' For him, life was always marked by new things, by facts, encounters that became events."

The new group of young responsibles for CLU in Bologna lived with this level of intensity for years, in day to day life with Enzo, "side by side." It was an experience punctuated by their Monday meetings in the restaurant at Porta San Vitale. "Everything was judged and decided there," and nothing was ever taken for granted.

Among the many incidents that show this zeal for life, Elena recalls one case that took place when she was in her third year of studies at the College of Letters. "There was a student strike at the university and I had stayed home in my apartment to study. Enzo called unexpectedly, and said, 'Do you see how the freshmen are doing your work for you? They're standing in front of the gate of the College of Letters, doing battle with the leftist extremists trying to get in. Meanwhile, you're sleeping!' I ran to the college right away. Once again, Enzo was asking me to change, to look at reality, at what new things were happening."

Over the years, Enzo's leadership gradually grew stronger and his companionship more binding, while the CLU community was growing around the new group of young responsibles, reaching a size of over fifteen hundred members. It was and it remains one of the most important and active entities among all the universities in Italy.

"Along this path," Cristina relates, "Enzo was a point of reference, of unity, of comparison for us, and meetings with him were always a place to think out loud, to bring personal questions and questions about the community out into the open, to set out toward renewed goals, to become entirely united with the thoughts of Father Giussani and of the universal Church. Enzo never offered us a one on one and exclusive relationship; he always created places of unity where we could grow—an overwhelming unity, with those phone calls, even at night: 'News?' You were always unprepared in the face of this question, never able to respond in kind. The answers, the right ones, would always come later, once you hung up the receiver, while his question would linger like a worm inside you."

Enzo stood alongside his kids in all the vicissitudes of life, even when sorrow would enter the story of family ties. "You would find him at your grandfather's funeral, with time for a hug and an assignment: 'Stay close to your grandmother and your mom.'"

He was tireless in this educational task, beyond all human strength. So much so that Cristina asks the question, "Didn't Enzo ever sleep?" She adds, "He was always on the run, but never out of breath. Phone calls, quick meetings to address sensitive and urgent issues, then in the evening after a hard day's work he would find time to go and visit a friend. If we put it all together and made out a list, you would doubt that a single man could take on such an undertaking with so broad a sweep.

"One day after a meeting," Cristina concludes, "I told him, 'For me, love for Christ comes after love for people, because I have such a strong desire not to lose them.' He answered, 'Yes, it is a road, a longer road. For me, Christ comes first.' What he said—you could reach out and touch it in the way he lived. We never saw a single moment, not even on vacation, or at home, or behind the wheel of his car, we never saw him living a single instant without this pull toward affirming Christ, who would show himself in all his beauty and strength through Enzo."

"In those years, the group of university responsibles in Bologna," writes Massimo Camisasca,[3] "made an important contribution to the life of the whole Movement, both in terms of the credence Piccinini gained in leading CL in Italy, and in the vitality of the Bolognese phenomenon."

Beginning in the mid-eighties, Enzo became part of the National Council of Communion and Liberation and Father Giussani assigned him the task of being the visitor to one of the three broad areas that the Movement was divided

---

3. Massimo Camisasca, *Communion and Liberation: The Recognition*, op. cit. 69–70.

into in Italy, the one which comprised the three Veneto regions and the Adriatic coast, running from Padua down to Lecce, including Basilicata. In those days there were more than twenty thousand CL members gathered into dozens and dozens of communities, some in small towns, in the provinces assigned to Piccinini.

Enzo's new responsibilities had him travelling thousands of miles from the north of Italy to the south, engaged in a tireless flurry of relationships, producing a change in every locality and good fruits that remain to this day. This is how he described it: "Father Giussani cannot visit all the places where the Movement exists, so he chose a few people who are very close to him and who go everywhere, doing what he would do."

In order to understand more fully the significance of this new assignment, Enzo went along with Giussani on his visit to several houses of the Memores Domini.[4] "When we came to the first house," Enzo recounted, "Father Giussani rang the doorbell, and when they answered him on the intercom he said, 'Excuse me, it's Father Giussani; I don't mean to bother you. Our meeting was supposed to be Wednesday, but I wanted to ask if we could do it today.' He said it exactly like this: 'Excuse me, I don't mean to bother you.' I thought, if he had come to my house I would have thrown all the doors open! Later, when the meeting began, it was extraordinary to hear him speak. Father Giussani knew every one of them, each one by name, and would ask things like, 'How's your dad? Is he taking his medication?' There was a bond between them, an affection I had never seen before."

After visiting the various houses, Father Giussani asked Piccinini, "Do you understand?"

"I'm beginning to understand," Enzo replied. "Basically, being a visitor means belonging to the Movement, loving everything and doing everything with this belonging alive in your heart and in your mind, with this capacity for connection that is called fatherhood. What the visitor needs to do is to make sure that every relationship is kept as an open wound, a wound which is known as conversion."

"This is how the Movement is born for us, as new relationships," Enzo explained. "It's how the Movement stays new, as an intense experience that with one stroke wipes away all divisions. The point is that I convert, and that we help one another so conversion can happen. Over time, this is what bears outstanding fruit."

This is the way Piccinini lived his task of being a visitor from the very start, not by acting out a role, but by reverencing it as an opportunity for his own conversion. As his responsibilities grew, he threw his heart wide open and

---

4. Memores Domini [Latin: "Those who recall the Lord"] is an ecclesial association which sprang from the Movement of Communion and Liberation, and is commonly known as the *Gruppo adulto* [the Grownup Group]. The Memores live a total dedication to Christ and to the Church in chastity, obedience, and poverty, seeking to establish a missionary presence in the various fields of employment.

wanted every action to involve the whole world, as "the *tour de force* of the infinite." "This is why," he would say, "we get up every morning: to help Christ save the world, with whatever strength we have, with whatever light we possess, asking Christ to give us more light and more strength." His CL friends from Puglia, one of the regions entrusted to his care as visitor, remember him in this way: "Piccinini irresistibly fascinated everyone who met him, because he was a spectacular example of a man: he loved his work, his patients, his friends; he travelled the world to help the Movement and to learn his profession; he liked good whiskey and good cigars, he was interested in politics, and he played soccer. He taught us a Spanish song that he really liked, which says, 'Give us a big heart to love; give us a strong heart to fight.'[5] That's what he was like, with his reason and his responsibility always ready to affirm what he had recognized as true, never letting up. He gave a big gift to our region; he begot a history of men with a passion for life and for the destiny of all."

In 1997, after returning from a study trip in Taiwan, his daughter Chiara often went along with Enzo in his travels. "He would cover half of Italy in a week. I was amazed at his endurance; he never seemed tired. He would come to the communities and hold meetings, all charged up and full of energy, as if he had done nothing but sleep on the way there. My father was always outside the box, trying to help people grow by prodding them to get moving, but then he would walk every step with anyone who accepted his challenge."

"I remember when Enzo used to come visit our community," adds Giuseppe. "He never wasted a minute. Everything was focused and full of meaning; not a word was spoken at random, to the point that I sometimes felt like saying, 'Give us a chance to breathe!' It was all of extreme importance, including the soccer game. Passion for life, born from his relationship with Father Giussani, dominated everything."

Part of Enzo's responsibility was maintaining close relationships with the heads of various ecclesiastical entities, primarily in Bologna, first with Archbishop Enrico Manfredini, then, after his sudden death in December of 1983, with Cardinal Giacomo Biffi. But he was also esteemed in other dioceses. In 1999, His Excellency Carlo Caffarra, then bishop of Ferrara, invited him to share his witness, acknowledging him as one of the most influential contributors to the life of the Church in Italy. That same year he was invited to Pesaro, and His Excellency Angelo Bagnasco, then bishop of that city, remembered Enzo after his death with "the affection of a father and a shepherd."

Within Enzo, Father Giussani's fatherhood had stirred a living love for the life of the Church, even in its institutions. Widmer remembers a significant episode which demonstrates this love.

"Piccinini had accompanied Father Giussani on his visit to the Cardinal of Bologna, Giacomo Biffi. When His Eminence became their meeting, Father

---

5. In the original Spanish of this song, entitled *"Danos un corazón,"* these lines are as follows: *"Danos un corazón grande para amar; danos un corazón fuerte para luchar."*

Giussani suddenly kissed his ring. Enzo did too, but a little awkwardly and with little conviction. "Cardinal Biffi, keenly noting the difference in attitude, said to Father Giussani, whom he had known well since their years of priestly formation in the seminary of Venegono, 'See, he'll do it, but he doesn't believe in it.' Father Giussani answered, 'True, but if he keeps on doing it, he will eventually believe in it.'

"Father Giussani's prophecy came true. In the months before his death, Enzo lavished all his energy on helping to organize the Eucharistic Congress in Bologna, where Pope John Paul II also took part. Piccinini involved the whole community in this undertaking, especially university students. This is the sign that an affection for the Church, even in its institutional aspect, had blossomed in his life, and this affection can only be understood in light of his obedience to Father Giussani."

Enzo was very struck, to the point of being moved, by a verse from Isaiah that he would often quote: "Behold, I have engraved you on the palms of my hands."[6] "He explained to me," continues Widmer, "that when he went to school, he used to write crib notes on his palms so he could copy them down. He wrote only the most important things. So he was moved by the thought that God had put his name on the palms of his hands, as something important. For Enzo, Giussani was a father who had drawn him on the palms of the hands. In front of don Giuss, Piccinini, who as you know was a man of strong character and brimming with self-esteem, would suddenly become like a child, with that complete ingenuousness that characterizes them: everything from Giussani and everything for Giussani. His every action, activity, and decision affirmed this personal connection with the charism that had begotten him for Christ and that increasingly led him to the root of the Mystery who makes all things. Enzo would look at Father Giussani and would identify with him, bringing along with him the extraordinary strength of his talents. He didn't need to quote phrases from don Giuss, because everything corresponded to this connection that he had attracted. And just as he saw don Giuss acting like a father toward him, so he acted toward us, constantly struggling against his character limitations, which were sometimes blatant, but which never managed to keep him from being a father."

---

6. Isaiah 49:16.

Chapter Four
Sacrum facere[1]

Enzo had scheduled a surgery at the San Lorenzino Care Center in Cesena where he collaborated. On that afternoon of March 12, 1999, the operation was expected to be of average duration, and not particularly difficult, partly because on the morning of that same day Piccinini had had a challenging surgical shift at the Sant'Orsola-Malpighi Polyclinic in Bologna. During the surgery at the care center, however, it became clear that there were conditions calling for a more radical operation which would be much more beneficial to the patient. The decision was made to go ahead with the longer operation, even though it would take significantly more time.

"Piccinini performed the operation with great skill," recalls Raffaele, surgeon and director of the San Lorenzino Care Center. "It was not the kind of operation typical for our facility, but thanks to his capability, everything went in the best possible way. Still today, ten years later, the patient is grateful for that operation and its positive results."

But there was a problem. At nine in the evening on that same day, a public meeting was scheduled in Cesena entitled "The Patient: A Person, Not an Ailment," where Enzo was supposed to give his witness. Seeing that the operation was taking more time than anyone had expected, and aware of the inevitable fatigue that Enzo no doubt felt after having been entrenched in the operating room since morning, Raffaele suggested to his colleague that he postpone the meeting. Enzo firmly rejected this suggestion: the conference went ahead that evening as planned.

"It was a fantastic moment," continues Raffaele. "The room was full of doctors and nurses, many of whom were listening to Enzo for the first time. He was extremely tired, but as he spoke he seemed to regain his strength, so great was his desire to communicate the experience that lay at the origin of his passion for the surgical profession. It was not a theoretical discourse. There were no great definitions about the meaning of suffering or professional ethics. It was the

---

1. Latin for "to sacrifice," literally meaning "to make holy."

story of his life, of people he had met, of relationships that had begun, of life's most significant events. When at the end of his speech Enzo said that everything he did, he did in order that the human glory of Christ could be known in the world, his affirmation did not seem like a religious conclusion tacked on to abstract principles. It was clear to everyone that this was the real origin of what they had heard and seen in him.

"That evening, when I spoke to him as he was getting in his car to go back to Modena, with plans to go to Lecce the next day, as if struck by a strange premonition of what would happen next, I said, 'Enzo, be careful, because. . . .' Then I stopped myself, suddenly interrupted by a sort of embarrassment, but I had wanted to say, '. . . because we love you.' I remember Enzo's smile, which made me realize that he had guessed what I was thinking. He said nothing, but he raised his arms and looked up."

This is Raffaele's account of a portion of Enzo's professional life, hours and hours with his surgical instruments, with a clear awareness of the meaning of what he did, of why he did it, and his desire to talk about it, to share it: "Enzo helped me to overcome a sort of weariness, a full-blown lack of enthusiasm that had taken hold of me, especially when it came to work. Anyone who met him immediately sensed that he wanted to enter into dialogue not with your ideas, but with the experience that you were living as a human being."

Enzo was an expert surgeon, meticulous, scrupulous, and careful, but courageous when called for. He was a true leader who knew how to win the cooperation of his assistants, the anesthesiologists and the operating room nurses. He knew how to encourage his patients and he would always try to go above and beyond for them. He would go as far as he could, taking responsibility for everything. However, it was not always easy to have a relationship with him: "After an operation, he would not allow discussions about his surgical technique or his decisions."

"I still wonder how I was able, in spite of everything, to immediately forgive Enzo for certain aspects of his character," continues Raffaele. "The answer is that I saw in him an extraordinary and human passion for the destiny of the patient under his care. This factor, which amazed me, was so imposing that it overshadowed other aspects of his strong personality, which instinctively I would not have accepted."

In memory of that friendship and of his professional collaboration, the classroom of the San Lorenzino Care Center in Cesena where workshops and updates are held for doctors and paramedics is now named after Enzo.

The way Doctor Piccinini lived his profession struck everyone who met him. On this subject, Giorgio asserts that "the work of a surgeon requires profound attention, total dedication, a total capacity to focus on details. It can't be faked. You can't be in one place with your mind somewhere else. Enzo's professional skill was what it was because there was a profound unity between the various aspects of his busy life. This unity came from a presence that he recognized, from his perception of Someone else who was present in all circumstances. So he lived his involvement with the Movement of Communion and Liberation first of all as a loyalty toward his work, and also as a refreshment, as a desire for constant improvement, as a way of plunging into reality. In this sense, his friendship with Father Luigi Giussani made him more professional, more worldly, more involved in reality than the rest of his colleagues."

Enzo himself recognized this stamp that had been impressed upon him even in his professional life by his belonging to the Movement, and he would talk about it, recounting a conference that took place in Bari on the World Day of the Sick: "In my address I explained the structure of my surgical unit, our weekly meetings, both the technical ones and the ones where we look at how we treat the sick. I explained my work method, the internal functioning of the group, the sense of authority, of gravitas. At the end they even applauded me. Then someone stood up and asked me, 'Where did you learn all these things? Is there a place where they can be learned concisely and quickly?'

"I responded by talking about my course of formation, about what I learned outside of Italy, in the United States of America, in England. But the person who had asked the question kept insisting, 'Is there someplace where these things can be learned in a concise way?' Standing in front of the audience of that great hospital, when really everyone was there, surgeons, nurses, administration, I said, 'I know that this can raise many questions, but for me, it was a certain Father Giussani who taught me to be a surgeon.' Think about their reaction! They must have all thought, 'This guy is crazy.'

"So I said, 'Giussani didn't teach me what techniques to use in the operating room; I learned these on my own. But he taught me a position as a human being whereby my way of using technology is different, my way of treating the sick is different, my way of relating to others is different. This is where my passion comes from, from the fact that I was caught up in an adventure of this sort."

Piccinini's qualities were recognized by fellow surgeons not only in Italy, but also abroad. In him, they saw a new way of living their profession. Such is the case with Doctor Lodovico, whom Enzo had met during a trip to Florida, at a dinner held to introduce the Italian surgeon to members of the Country Club.

"That night I tried to irritate Enzo, for very personal reasons," recalls Lodovico. "I was hostile to the communities created by Father Giussani, and I did my best to highlight this disagreement. A sign of Piccinini's richness as a human being was the fact that instead of blowing me off, he sought me out later, precisely because of my hostility. He wanted to show me the reality of CL, who its members were and what they did. So we began a relationship based on friendship and respect and no longer on prejudice.

"I always admired his energy. He would travel from Italy to America, he would go back to Bologna, operate for ten hours, and hurry off to Milan. It was hard not to see a sign of the Spirit in Enzo's activity. He never got discouraged, even when things didn't go as he wished. I think he may have debunked one of the most destructive myths of our time, namely, that to succeed we have to achieve a predetermined goal. His success stemmed from his awareness of having a vocation, a mission. All the events of his life, even the apparent failures, were an opportunity to answer a call. I never understood as I did when looking at Enzo the meaning of the word sacrifice, from *sacrum facere*, to make holy, that is, set aside for a single purpose.

"In his work as a surgeon," Lodovico continues, "what most struck me was his desire for perfection. One of the reasons why I reconciled with CL is that I appreciated the impact that the Movement had on his desire for professional improvement. For his coworkers, Enzo had created the same sort of opportunities for professional satisfaction that had brought me to America."

Because of his respect for human dignity, Piccinini was convinced that patients had the right to know the truth about their illnesses and about impending death. "The so-called conspiracy of silence surrounding the dying, incorrectly understood as a form of compassion," Lodovico concludes, "is nothing but a preference for lies over truth, the ultimate expression of a lack of confidence in life. But for Enzo, what really mattered was the sacredness, the uniqueness of the human person."

Susanna worked a long time at Doctor Piccinini's side, first during her internship as a student, then in her five years of specialization in surgery at the Sant'Orsola-Malpighi Polyclinic. "Enzo used to demand that we have a special attention for the patient, that we always keep track of him—not only during surgery and after the operation, but also when, from the surgical point of view, nothing more could be done. We still had to be available. Enzo asked us for a total involvement and he motivated us toward this kind of behavior. He was a great communicator, and was able to establish a superb rapport with his patients. He would tell them the risks they were facing, but would add that the battle would be fought together. His involvement as a person gave a lot of courage to the sick and to their family members, who no longer felt alone. He would say, 'We have a problem, but you are not facing it alone; I'm here, and so are my coworkers.' In situations where others would give up in the end, he would never give up, and many times he was right to go ahead with his efforts."

Piccinini explained in these words how involvement with his patients had come in "with a crash" from the recognition of a common need and a shared question: "Sickness, suffering, pain, and death are the normal but sharpest expressions of human limitation, and the fact that man is limited can never be removed from one's awareness of life. This awareness leads to an otherwise impossible capacity for relationship. The sense of limitation immediately puts you next to others, even if they don't agree with you, even if they don't understand or even look at you. Because, just like them, you are needy. This awareness, which seems like a strange sentence, immediately forms an opening, because we understand with a crash that we're together, not because we think about it in the same way, but because we are needy in the same way. It is crucial to keep this in mind when we are with the sick. What an amazing patience comes from it! What an amazing renewal! There is no need to theorize about service; you start to do it for real."

The Piccinini Foundation recently received a testimony from South America. Carla, a new doctor, read the text of a speech in which Enzo talked about his experience, and she discovered a new and more authentic way to be a physician. She was saddened to see "indifference and resignation" in the local clinic where she was working. "At best, there might be an even passionate commitment to work, to the clinical case, to the laboratory results, to postoperative care, to the ability of antibiotics, but not to the person."

Carla was deeply surprised to read the words of Enzo, a doctor, a surgeon who claimed to be happy. "The doctors that I know are rarely happy." She was even more surprised that for Piccinini, happiness did not depend on his success, but rather on his involvement with the patient, not as a clinical case, but "as a person."

"From my environment, I had absorbed the idea that I had to know how to do everything. I found the attitude that you had to entrust yourself to something much bigger than yourself to be deeply genuine. The mistake is seeing the other person's life as if it depended only on me," concludes Carla. "It was wonderful news to know that I don't have to remove my humanity in order to be a doctor. This was the opposite of what I had been taught. I have to get involved, to put all my heart into it, or I am in danger of becoming cynical. I was only twenty and I was already starting to be cynical. But when you discover that it is possible to live this way, it's like beginning to breathe again."

After graduating under Piccinini, then doing surgical research at the University of Bologna, Giampaolo was the first specialization student to join the group of young doctors that Enzo was forming at the Sant'Orsola-Malpighi Polyclinic in 1990. Giampaolo, who continues to practice as a surgeon in the department once headed by Piccinini, together with "Enzo's group" and following the method taught by their teacher, remembers having in that period "a familiarity in relationships and a passion for keeping track of patients that was tangibly new."

"Enzo turned the normal way that surgeons deal with their patients upside down. In our profession you can easily end up feeling sort of omnipotent, thinking of yourself as capable of very delicate and complex operations that can solve the patient's problems. And so there's a temptation to treat patients with a certain detachment, without listening to them, because the doctor already knows what to do. But between Enzo and his patients I would see right from the start a level of familiarity that amazed me, that was not formal, not a façade.

"Even the patients' family members were aware that in Piccinini, they had met not only a superb surgeon who had the technical expertise to solve problems, but also a man who stood by their side and would share the dramatic experience of illness with them. They could count on Enzo. This was especially obvious in the most desperate cases.

"When you are faced with severe but operable maladies, where it is likely that everything will be fine," continues Giampaolo, "it is relatively easy to be a surgeon. But staying in front of the patient becomes much more difficult when the situation becomes more complicated, if the patient's life is in grave danger, if you see that there are no more easy ways out. Usually in these cases the surgeon tends to step back, because it is not easy for him to stay in front of his own limitations and recognize that we cannot solve everything with our hands.

"With Enzo, on the other hand, precisely in the most complicated situations, what came into view was the depth of the relationship that had been established between him and the patient and his family. I saw that, even when it was not possible to save the lives of patients, their families were just as grateful to Enzo for his openness to them, for how he had helped them by showing them, for example, how to stand alongside their loved ones in the last months of life with more truth, how to fully enjoy the relationship they had. Piccinini always used to say that sickness is an excruciating event for the person suffering it, but the hardest thing is not being able to experience sickness in a truly human way."

In his relationship with his students, Piccinini discarded teaching methods that were then widespread, where the expert surgeon tended to keep the skills he had acquired to himself as secrets of the trade. Enzo, on the contrary, "was not stingy with what he knew"; he was not afraid to share it, and in fact he made every effort to promote the professional growth of his students by having them not only listen and watch, but also operate, following a teaching model he had learned in the United States. He urged his students to go abroad to gain experience at university centers of excellence such as Harvard University, the University of Chicago, the Pierre and Marie Curie University in Paris, with which he maintained a continuing relationship. Piccinini supported these initiatives and endeavored to find resources for scholarships. In 1999 he advanced the creation of a master's degree in coloproctology sponsored by the European Union and by the University of Bologna, in collaboration with the Universities of Vienna and Madrid.

Passion for man and love for his destiny also made Enzo more attentive to scientific research as a way to better understand man and to improve his life; he promoted research projects with brilliant insight. One such case, a very meaningful one, involves a friendship that was the basis of a scientific project that is still ongoing. When Pierluigi, a new graduate from Bologna, told Enzo that an opportunity had unexpectedly opened up for him to continue working at the university as a researcher, Piccinini responded with three words: "So do research."

"It was no joke," says Pierluigi. "Enzo passed on some ideas to me that have been fundamental to my work. He strongly believed in researching molecular markers that could aid in the early detection of cancer. By that time he had become a nationally renowned cancer surgeon, and his professional training was of the highest level. He would handle cases which were considered to be very serious or incurable elsewhere. His patients came from all over Italy, and he would accompany them throughout the course of their treatment, which, given the seriousness of their cases, might not even be beneficial, but it often was, beyond all expectation.

"Piccinini had the idea that if he had been able to see these patients earlier, if there had been an early diagnosis, he would have been able to treat them more effectively. However, they sometimes came to him when it was too late. Enzo was convinced that, over a period of time, the identification of these molecular markers would reshape his own work as a surgeon, allowing for less invasive treatments."

The positive attitude with which Piccinini used to tackle every problem was fundamental to Pierluigi's professional path as a university researcher. "Enzo was convinced that if a problem has a solution, then the hypothesis that there is a solution will help us to find it. On the other hand, if you assume that there is nothing to be done, the solution will never be found."

"Led by his attitude and by his insight on molecular markers," Pierluigi continues, "I gathered other people around me and I started a new line of molecular research on cancer. Enzo helped us from the financial point of view as well, giving us suggestions about how to find resources, because this line of research is very expensive. When Enzo left us in May of 1999, we were stunned for a while. But the positive idea that he had indicated for us has always remained."

The research hypothesis that Piccinini suggested is that a tumor, even in its early stages, leaves traces in the blood cells. The work that was undertaken by Pierluigi and his companions aims to identify these traces and to develop a method to recognize them in a systematic way. Studies have shown that there is at least a technical possibility to initiate such procedures. The future prospect that could be achieved is particularly interesting: by means of a simple blood test, which would become routine, it could be possible to look for these markers and identify the molecules that indicate the beginning presence of a tumor when the subject is still well.

"We have already published several texts internationally and we are valued for the originality of our approach to the problem," concludes Pierluigi. "We are enthusiastically moving ahead with the hypothesis that Piccinini suggested, as if he were still here working with us."

Enzo's passion for education and his commitment to young university students also led to professional careers in fields other than health care and research. Among the many CL groups on college campuses in Italy, Enzo also used to serve as visitor to the university community of Pescara. In 1990, their local university was occupied by left-wing students, and the members of CLU engaged in a bitter struggle with them to convince them to stage an "intelligent occupation," that is, one that would allow examinations to be held. Giuseppe, who took up his position at the flank of the Catholic students during one heated assembly, was invited that same afternoon to a meeting with Piccinini on the Pescara university campus.

"I went," recalls Giuseppe, who was then twenty years old, "and I was shocked because I heard Enzo speaking about desire as the thing that drives the I." At the end of the meeting, Piccinini was introduced to the young university student, who told him about his passion for sports; in fact, Giuseppe was the Italian champion in karate. On subsequent trips to Pescara Enzo always inquired about how his matches were going.

Thus was born a friendship. "When I spoke with Enzo I understood that destiny stood in our midst. He taught me the sacredness of desire as a gift of my humanity." Giuseppe attended the College of Economics and had a passion for mechanics. After an examination on the technology of production cycles he told Piccinini that this subject had become very interesting to him. "Enzo said, 'If I were you, I would try to understand why and what it means that this exam struck you.' He said it to me in such a serious way that a few days later I went to talk to my technology professor." This is what led Giuseppe to write a thesis on industrial automation and to obtain a further master's degree in the economics of technological innovation in the U.S. "That's what Enzo was like; he would always encourage you. He would say, 'Go!'"

"Fresh out of college," Giuseppe concludes his story, "I did the military service, and to please my parents, I took part in a competition at that time to be given a position at the Bank of Italy, and I won. At the same time, however, another opportunity was developing. Thanks to the studies I had done (I had specialized in the revitalization of companies in crisis), I was invited to get involved in a metal engineering company that was experiencing difficulties. I was supposed to finalize the restructuring plan and, if I brought it to a successful conclusion, I would be hired as the business director of the company. My parents and my friends suggested that I choose a secure position with the Bank of Italy. I talked about it with Enzo. He didn't tell me what to choose, as others did, but he said that I had to consider the passion I had inside and try to understand what the Mystery was asking of me."

Giuseppe thus decided to work for the metal engineering company, which returned to optimum levels after just three years. At the same time another opportunity appeared to help a company burdened with three million dollars of debt.

"Once again, my friends were telling me, 'Who would tell you to go there? You're already an executive; you have a good salary.' But I continued to look for an answer: Why had I come across this company? Why did I discern this opportunity? Enzo said, 'I don't know how it will come out, but know that you're worthwhile, because you are a relationship with the Mystery who is present. God does not give you a skill for you to go do something else; however, you're the one who has to decide.' At that point I took in a deep breath."

Now the company is a leading business with four hundred employees, including one hundred abroad, and a research center collaborating with the University.

Chapter Five
Face to Face with Destiny

The flight from New York had just landed at Malpensa. Getting off the plane, on May 26, 1999, Alberto turned on his mobile phone. The first call came after a few minutes. It was not yet nine in the morning.

"I don't know why, but last night Enzo didn't come home. He was in Milan for a supper with the Center of CLU. He left after supper, but he never got back home."

Alberto was returning from the UN, where two days earlier, on May 24, Father Luigi Giussani's volume *At the Origin of the Christian Claim*, the English translation of *All'origine della pretesa cristiana* had been presented.

"I spoke with Enzo yesterday," said Alberto. "He was looking for me because he wanted to know every detail about how it had gone at the UN. I told him. Have you tried checking the hospital? Sometimes when he gets back late and has to operate early in the morning, he goes straight to Sant'Orsola to sleep."

"Nobody's seen him at the hospital either. But—I don't know how to tell you—along the freeway near Fidenza, the police found a car on the side of the road that burned up in a collision with a bridge embankment. There was a charred body inside. It all looks like it might be Enzo."

"No! Let's hope not. God forbid! But when you have news let me know right away."

The second call confirming Enzo's tragic death was not long in coming. The identification was made after a briefcase containing some of his documents was found.

Alberto recounts, "I immediately called Father Giussani, who was in his house at Gudo Gambaredo. I struggled to give him the terrible news, partly because when he picked up he thought the reason for my call was to tell him how the book presentation had gone at the UN. But no. . . . Giussani paused silently for a long time, and then said, 'Alberto, do you think you could come here? Sometimes it's better to be with friends.' He also asked me to inform other people in Milan and Bologna right away."

Alberto will never forget Father Luigi Giussani's face when he arrived. "He was distraught, like when your dearest friend dies. Enzo was a favorite son for him. Giussani was a father to Enzo; he had snatched him from a road where he would have been lost. He had awakened in him, partly because of their remarkable affinity of temperament, enthusiasm for Christ, for faith, as the all-embracing content of life, family, work, relationships, and responsibility for the Movement. It was an enthusiasm that Enzo acted on with everything and everyone, from greatest to least, down to the rawest rookie."

In the great hall of the house at Gudo Gambaredo Alberto remained silent for a moment, then said, "The only thing that comes to mind, faced with this immense pain, is the cross and resurrection." Giussani answered, "Without the awareness of the resurrection the cross cannot be carried. It is unsustainable."

"As time went on," Alberto continues his story, "we were joined by other friends. Giussani was deeply wounded by this great trial that the Mystery had given him, but in dealing with us, he had a clear conviction that the legacy Enzo had left behind had to be carried on. Enzo's death had occurred so that we could become more aware of our identity. In particular, he told some of our friends from Bologna that the magnitude of the task carried out by Enzo in those years could be carried on only through their unity."

On that morning of May 26, 1999, the news of Enzo's sudden death reached thousands of friends throughout Italy by telephone. This is how the news reached his daughter, Anna Rita, while she was attending class at the College of Medicine at the University of Bologna.

"Betta came to get me," relates Anna Rita, "telling me to leave the classroom quickly. We had to leave for Milan because Father Giussani urgently needed to talk with me. Then, when we were all in the car, Daniela told me what had happened. My legs were shaking; I felt like I had no more strength. I had seen my dad for the last time two days earlier. It's a beautiful memory. He was wearing a white shirt. The previous Sunday he had been walking on Monte Cusna with a group of friends. It was sunny and he got a tan from walking outside. We hugged when we left. Then on May 25 I had stopped by to greet him in his office in the ward, but he wasn't there because he was operating. So I wrote him a note and I left it on his desk, thinking that he would read it after the surgery." But Enzo came out of the operating room late that evening, and immediately left for Milan without visiting his office. His daughter's note stayed on his desk, where his colleagues found it the next day.

When Anna Rita reached Milan, Father Giussani was crying. Fiorisa and the other children were already with him. Don Giuss said to them, "Do us the charity of thinking of us as your family from now on."

"I took those words literally," continues Anna Rita. "I remember that for the next few days I did not want to go back to Bologna anymore, where everything reminded me of Enzo; then my friends helped me, and when I passed the first exam I telephoned Father Giussani, as I used to do with my dad. He said, 'Come up and see me.' Through Enzo's sacrifice, I found Jesus Christ in the real embrace of blossoming friendships—a gratuitous love for me, for my life, from those who are close to me, who ask nothing in return. I felt and I feel the emptiness. I felt and I feel the pain of the wound. But I'm beginning to see the fruit. This incomprehensible thing does have a meaning."

On that same day, along with Alberto, Fiorisa and her children Anna Rita, Chiara, Pietro, and Maria who had gathered around Father Giussani, other friends from Milan, Bologna and other cities also came. Among them was Widmer, who had been with Enzo, three days before he died, during a hike on Monte Cusna, a mountain that Enzo loved, located in the Apennines in the province of Reggio Emilia. Today, on top of that mountain, there is a plaque placed there by the university students of Bologna in memory of their friend "who so loved this mountain and our freedom."

"Being our guide on Cusna," Widmer recounts, "was his way of making us understand that the path of faith is difficult. But in companionship, we conquer something even bigger, one step at a time." Some time earlier, Enzo had expressed this idea with the metaphor of a hot air balloon, which as it rises—that is, as one goes deeper into the experience of Christianity—the horizon is constantly growing wider.

"The news of Enzo's death," continues Widmer, "reached me through a call to my cell phone while I was on the train on my way back to Milan. I went through a moment of complete disorientation. Then questions began to crowd into my mind: 'What kind of a business is God running? Doesn't he realize that his company is in crisis? How can you let go of those who bring home the most significant results? What will happen to the inheritance of faith that the world is so lacking?'"

Widmer arrived, his heart laden with pain and with these questions that he could not answer. Then, meeting with Father Luigi Giussani, he understood that "God does not want the faith to diminish. So if a friend disappears, another one has to take on the responsibility of ensuring that this inheritance will remain in the world."

"It was one of the most provocative and decisive things I have ever heard, because it lies at the basis of my conversion."

Luigi was also a part of that group of friends who climbed to the top of Monte Cusna on May 23, 1999. On their way down they had fun sliding along some ravines which still had snow. Then they ate lunch—grilled fish—and spent a good long time at table, enjoying what the operator of a trout farm at the foot of the mountain had prepared for Enzo and his friends.

It was a joyful, sunny day, as they enjoyed the beauty of being together, one of the many days that Enzo would organize on the spur of the moment with a round of telephone calls: "So, on Sunday let's go to Cusna."

"In the afternoon," says Luigi, "we said goodbye for the last time in the parking lot of a gas station along the road from Modena to Sassuolo. I still have a vivid memory of Enzo, as he drove his car away into the distance. When I learned that his earthly journey had ended in the arms of Christ, I started to pray to him, asking for his help, reading and rereading what he had written. I catch myself wondering, 'What would Enzo be doing if he were still with us now?' I feel his presence. He is present. I can't call him on the phone, but the essence doesn't change. I'm as grateful to him now as I was then."

Davide also mourns his deceased friend: "After Enzo, on behalf of Father Luigi Giussani, took on the duties of visitor to the communities of Communion and Liberation in Veneto, Emilia Romagna and the Adriatic coast, it became more difficult to talk with him. So some friends and I insisted that he give us some time to help us face an urgent problem together. That was the last time we met and Enzo, as he said goodbye to us, took me aside and said, 'Look, Davide, I don't know the future, but one thing's for sure: you and I will always be here to serve the Movement and the Church. Maybe we'll be sacristans when we're old, but we will always be here.'

"They gave me the awful news by phone, while I was in the outpatient clinic. 'Dead?' 'Yes, dead.' There followed a minute of heavy silence; then I went to Milan to be with Giussani. It seemed impossible that the space and time of life could be deprived of his presence, which had filled so many days, which had drawn my attention, which had directed my energies. But in reality I have realized that his death was not really a death for me. I've always felt him present, maybe because I had to decide for myself, wondering what God was asking of me through that event. Enzo was a sign chosen by the Mystery so that the eyes of many people could be opened. His presence is still working through the certainty of those who met him and were educated, made certain, more certain through him."

"Up to the day of Enzo's death, followed soon after by Emilia's," Giorgio adds, "I was somehow convinced that those who lived the Christian experience in such an all-encompassing way, as they did, would be preserved from the conditions affecting others, as if they were defended by some sort of magic. But then I realized that this adventure gives no concessions; it takes place in the normal conditions that everyone experiences, and the exceptional nature of faith does not confer privileges in terms of the conditions of life. Enzo's greatness unfolded in everyday life, subject to the limitations everyone suffers. These limitations increase the greatness and exalt the personality of the Christian. So ten years later his memory has not diminished, but is still growing."

Enzo had his last meal with his friends in a small restaurant in Milan. Gathered around the table were the seven national responsibles for Communion and Liberation in the universities. They met regularly, every three weeks, and would talk about everything that had to do with life in the various communities. Enzo wanted in a particular way to always be present every time they met.

On May 25, the conversation among those friends had gone on till midnight. Enzo's workday had begun early in the morning. There had been a long surgical procedure on his schedule. "We worked side by side all day in the operating room," Giampaolo recalls. "The last operation, however, lasted longer than expected. So he entrusted me with finishing the job because he had to leave for Milan. The following day, the hardest thing was going through the wards to tell each patient that Enzo had died, including those who were waiting to be operated on by him. One of them said, 'I'll only ask for one thing. I've been to many hospitals, but I've never seen a group like yours. I hope each of you can go to a different city to create something like what I've found here. Everyone who is sick like me should be able to experience what I have.'"

From that last supper in the little Milanese restaurant, what Father Pino remembers about Enzo is "the heartfelt tone of a father with which he spoke about the development of some rather difficult situations in some communities, naming names, describing the characters of the people involved, as if he were telling personal stories about his family. For him, other people were not problems, were not issues to be dealt with in a sociological way: they were persons, real faces. What absorbed him was the destiny of each person, and he would speak about them with precision, with accuracy, with a surprising attention to even the details and certain features of life. During that supper we talked for a long time about a community which had certain complex divisions. Enzo never settled for anything less than clarity of judgment, but at the same time he possessed an urgency, a sort of painful ache, that those friends could live the true experience of the Movement, not as an organization, but as the encounter with Christ alive and present. His charism came from a burning passion for the Lord that also showed itself as a burning passion for every person he met. Shortly after midnight we said goodnight. I offered him a Tuscan cigar. He jumped into his car and as usual peeled out as he drove away, like an expert driver."

When Enzo left from Milan, May 26 was just beginning. That night, less than an hour later, his destiny was mysteriously brought to completion along the freeway, near the Fidenza toll plaza. Weeks before the accident, he had had a premonition of what would happen.

His Excellency Carlo Caffarra, Cardinal of Bologna, recounts, "There's an incident that always comes to my mind when Enzo is mentioned, a mysterious conversation. A few days before his death, on May 14, 1999, he came to Ferrara to hold a conference at the Sala Estense.[1] This meeting was part of an event series to which I had invited, in the city where I was then bishop, certain great witnesses of Christ in the Italian Church to speak of their encounter with the Lord.

"Enzo had spoken of his journey of faith, and had admirably succeeded in making a synthesis between thinking about the encounter with Christ, bringing out Christianity's basic structure, and talking about it through the experience he lived. This fact had deeply impressed everyone present. Enzo knew how to show a proposal that is always very essential for life and that had became flesh and

---

1. The Sala Estense is a small theater located in Ferrara, built by a member of the noble Este family.

blood in him, and so was attractive. Whatever he talked about, it was never just talking theory. There was life in it. Every speech of his would always become a personal witness. A witness tells of facts, and forces you to say yes or no. Here lay the charism for education that he would bring to bear. One person who had taken part in that conference, a well-known professional, told me, 'I've tried for a lifetime to live Christianity, but tonight I realized that I have not yet understood a thing.'

"When we said goodbye, I said to Enzo, 'I would like to see you, nothing formal—just to spend some time as friends.' He replied, 'I'd really like that too. We'll be sure to do it. Unless,' he added, 'a few weeks from now you hear that Enzo died in a car accident.'

"I heard these words and I interpreted them in the sense that we believers, when we make an appointment beyond the day we are currently living, must always add, as Jesus teaches us, 'if God wills it.' I did not give those words any meaning other than that and certainly they did not have one.

"Later, when the news reached me about his death along the freeway, I remembered that conversation and I began to reflect. I thought that Enzo had an ongoing and watchful awareness of living for the Lord and thus of being completely at His disposal. I had never understood as I did then, thinking back to that encounter, the words of Saint Paul: 'Whether we live, whether we die, we belong to the Lord.' Later on I also thought that in these painful moments we see the back side of the embroidery. And the back side of an embroidery is always a big jumble. But we are certain that there is a design on the other side."

Some of the words spoken by Enzo in that meeting in Ferrara on May 14, 1999, just days before his death, lucidly explain what faith meant for him and how it impacted his whole life.

"The Christian position is the human position in the true sense of the word: outside of Christianity, the human being is incomplete. The experience of Christianity is the experience of humanity, and the Church is the teacher of this humanity. Christ is everything for man's life. Everything. There can be nothing in the life of a man who loves his own humanity loyally and to the end that can be held back from his relationship with Christ, because Christ is the heart of every man's life. I would not be part of the Christian experience were it not for this. I would also rebel against even the thought that being Christian means, as many think, being men who are a little less than others and with a few more problems. If I choose to stay here in the Christian experience, it's because it's here that I find myself, what I've always been looking for."

His Excellency Luigi Negri also has a clear memory of this intimacy with the Lord that Enzo spoke of in Ferrara: "In the last months of Enzo's life, as time went on, I sensed a deeper level of friendship with Christ growing in him. It was as if, on life's journey, staying inside this belonging and vigorously following his mission, as he did, was opening his life, in a way that was also amazing to him, to a personal encounter with the Lord, with His face. It's a mystical level that all Christians are destined to, but rarely get to, because it is so easy to get bogged down in moralism or sentimentality.

"I saw that, slowly but surely, Enzo's humanity and his Christianity were opening up to this intimacy with Christ. And the Lord dramatically expanded this beginning of intimacy by calling him to Himself, in a way that from a human point of view is so difficult to understand, in the searing event of his end on earth and his beginning in heaven.

"Since his death," continues Bishop Luigi Negri, "Enzo's voice no longer comes to us in the way of flesh and blood, and this is an agonizing rupture that each of us is careful to handle in a way that won't overwhelm us. The communion of saints is the only thing that allows us to live it with dignity, without despairing over death, whether our own or that of others, without despairing over the illnesses that strike us, without despairing over the evil that we do or that we suffer. The communion of saints says that our daily path is already touching the eternal now, and there is a fellowship that enlivens us, stirs us, and keeps us from closing ourselves in on the narrow horizon of our feelings or our resentments.

"Today we are called to recognize Enzo: not in the way of flesh and blood, not in the way of an embrace or a handshake, but in the mysterious but no less real way of faith. We recognize him present today in our midst, in a way that is mysterious but no less real than the short period of time when the Lord allowed us to be with him here."

Deeply affected by that "great pain," on May 26, 1999, Father Luigi Giussani wrote in a message to all the communities of CL in Italy and throughout the world, remembering his dear friend who was like a son to him, "This is certainly the worst pain with which God is testing our entire Fraternity at this time, because Enzo was a man who, from the intuition he gained in a conversation with me thirty years ago, said his yes to Christ with astounding dedication, with intelligence and an all-encompassing perspective, and made his whole life attached to Christ and to his Church. What most impressed me is that his adherence to Christ was so all-consuming that there was never a day when he would not seek out the human glory of Christ in every possible way.

"What is the mystery of God calling us to in such a trial of great suffering? He is asking us to always remember Christ as the meaning of life at all levels and in all areas: *Christ is all in all.* Thus it becomes clearer to us, over time, that salvation, that is, the positive affirmation of being, always implies the cross as its condition: *Ave crux, spes unica....*[2]

"It would not be rational if pain were not redeemed in the affirmation of Christ. This, my friends, is in any case the contradiction that nothing in the world can resolve. Faith in Christ is the only possibility of the peace and joy that the mystery of His Resurrection gives us in Him. So we also pray to Enzo to

---

2. From a Latin hymn: "Hail to the cross, our only hope."

help us remember all this, before the world can attack our heart and destroy all its positivity and thus all its hope."

Seven thousand friends from all over Italy packed the Basilica of San Petronio in Bologna for Holy Mass on the day of the funeral. The homily was delivered by Cardinal Giacomo Biffi, who was a personal friend of Enzo, and began with the words spoken by Jesus at the thought of that terrible hour that awaited him at the end of his earthly adventure: "My soul is troubled" (John 12:27), words that perfectly expressed the sentiment of those present in that "painful and unexpected" hour that they were going through.

"Faced with mystery of death," Cardinal Giacomo Biffi affirmed, "it is never possible for us, poor creatures cast into the riddle of existence, to overcome the anguish. Furthermore, it was not possible even for the Son of God." Anguish: "due to a pain that does not subside" over a "beloved brother suddenly seized by a merciless fate that in one stroke has cut short a precious and intense life, wiping out in an instant a legacy of extraordinary humanity, of spiritual riches, of unlimited dedication, of projects, of high resolutions. My soul is also troubled and suffers the loss of a friend, a friend in quiet and peaceful days and a friend in busy and hardworking days, a friend in days enlivened and consoled by the same ideal of effective witness to Christ and by our common belonging to the Church."

Then there is the question "Why?" that we address to the Lord, from whom it is natural "to demand an account for this death, which seems like a robbery," even if "we do not ask to understand, because there are some painful mysteries that no one is able to resolve for us here below." However, there is a saying of the Lord that "helps us to look forward with a trusting heart: 'Unless the grain of wheat fall to the ground and die, it remains alone; but if it dies, it bears much fruit' (John 12:24). God," Cardinal Giacomo Biffi concluded, "knows the roads that lead the lives of his little ones to a larger and more lasting fruitfulness and that transform our grief into a redemptive energy to the benefit of all our brothers. It is with this conviction that the apostle Paul can boldly write, 'In my flesh I complete what is lacking in Christ's afflictions for the sake of his body, that is, the Church' (Colossians 1:24). Today we bury in the furrows of this Emilian soil the mortal body of our friend Enzo. We bury him as a seed, that is, as a promise and an assurance of strengthened and expanded vitality for the communities of Communion and Liberation, for all our people, for the entire human family."

Each of the seven thousand friends who gathered in San Petronio carried a personal memory, a piece of living history with Enzo that had marked his life, as well as the question that Cardinal Biffi had asked in his homily: "Why?" Raffaele says, "The word 'pain' is not enough to describe what I felt then: I did not understand why the Lord had prematurely taken from us a person who was so generously giving his life for the glory of Christ on this earth. I could not understand why the great creative force that was in Enzo, which showed itself in a capacity to inspire work, was so cruelly cut short. Father Luigi Giussani helped us understand that we had to inquire what the Lord was asking of our lives through that dramatic fact. What the mystery was asking from us was to love Christ more and more.

"Faced with the death of our great friend, this was a first step toward leaving our bewilderment behind and regaining a position of faith. Taking this step, however, was not easy for me and could not be taken lightly."

Enzo's daughter Chiara, having come back from China, has this memory of Holy Mass in the Basilica of San Petronio on the day of the funeral: "I didn't see all the people who were behind me in church because I was in front, beside the coffin. But at the beginning, after the celebrant said, 'The Lord be with you,' the response 'And with your spirit' was loud and spoken together as if pronounced by one person. I felt that my father was not dead. He was no longer with us physically, but he left all the fruit of his labor, all those people, who in one way or another continued to support me."

Fiorisa was amazed and moved by the very many people she "did not recognize, nor had ever seen before" who in the subsequent weeks and months testified to their friendship with Enzo, relating how they felt him alive and present "in their memory and in their hearts." Andrea Aziani, who died in July 2008 in mission territory, was one of these people. "I too lost a friend just two years older than myself (I was born in '53)," he wrote, "but Enzo has never been as present in my life and in our lives here in Lima as he is today. Last night in our fraternity group we read one of his testimonies."

The dean of the University of Bologna, Fabio Roversi Monaco, recalled Piccinini, "the man, the teacher, the researcher," as "a true person—true in faith, in his university responsibility, in being a father and a man committed to doing good, and true when he would suddenly be incensed in the presence of injustice or of superficial or vulgar behavior."

His daughter Maria wrote to Father Luigi Giussani, "I wanted to tell you that when my friends gave me that extremely difficult news, I was infuriated, because the first thing I thought of was making every effort to save him, to bring him back, with an obvious and heartbreaking powerlessness and lack of means. The first thing you told me when we met was, 'He will accomplish more than before,' and then, 'He is more present than before.' I now have the impression, thinking back on many details, that everything had been meticulously prepared for his death. Everything: friends he had around him at work (where he reached his greatest success), in the university, in the Movement, in his family. Even the garden, which he carefully tended, had somehow reached perfection.

"Thanks to the amazing openness of my mom, lots of people came to see us or wrote to us, bringing thousands of testimonials on how Enzo had worked and struck people in every place and in every field. Some university students were like brothers for the way they shared this great pain with us, courageously and discreetly. There can no longer be half-measures for me when it comes to these people; our friendship can only be understood as a mission. What I want now is to tell everyone what happened, because miracles are happening here."

On the first anniversary of his death, May 26, 2000, Father Luigi Giussani remembered Enzo with these words: "When my poor mother, watching the last star in the morning sky, would say to me when I was a child, 'How beautiful is the world and how great is God,' she was at the threshold of consummation, the door to the goal, where everything becomes as clear as full dawn. Just one year ago Enzo completely and mysteriously crossed that threshold. He did so suddenly, but not naively. Every moment of his life, in fact, so pure and abandoned to Jesus—after the encounter that had transformed his structure, including some characteristics of his temperament, while enhancing others—was laid out in anticipation of the final consummation, like a walk in the fog through hardship and weakness, until the fog begins to glow because the sun comes out.

"Friends, we can say or do nothing unless we individually and jointly become accustomed to understanding this final passage, which is a pole of our present experience. For this, too, we must thank our friend Enzo. His stature as a man, impacted by the humanity of Jesus, was expanded, communicating itself with a crash to anyone he met, with that drive for living that characterized him and that we could not replicate—when he was absent, something was missing from our gatherings—such that it was immediately perceived by those who came across him for even a moment, whether a colleague or a patient—the impact of an exceptional presence, which rekindled hope, and so gave rise to the question about why he was like that. . . .

"Let us ask Enzo to help us walk from light to light, as even the great Eliot said, accepting everything for the glory of Jesus, so that we may, like him, be companions on the road to destiny for one another. For this was the secret of his fatherhood, so clearly seen in his family. Our great friend reminds us that nothing that exists is made to be destroyed, because Jesus is present; He is the ultimate structure of all things. In Him, in fact, all things consist, says Saint Paul. Let us ask Our Lady of the Rosary for the miracle of incorporating the forceful and tender humanity of this man who is our friend forever, so that the Church may live within our fragile bodies, in the strength of Him who is our joy."

That seed planted in the darkness of the earth and in the light of Christ has sprouted, has continued to bear fruit, and bears it more and more. Even the works that were generated by Enzo's creativity have not ceased.

In 2002, Massimo explains, a foundation to support and advance "the works that permanently testify to the beauty that was met and lived with Enzo in the areas where he gave his life" was established as the Enzo Piccinini Foundation, of which Massimo is president. "Our work is divided into different directions. First of all, we wish to document Enzo's life and works, collecting and sorting his writings, pictures of him, and testimonials about him in our archives. There is also a steady stream of letters coming to the Foundation from various parts of Italy and the world. They are expressions of gratitude for the encounter with Enzo, who has positively impacted the lives of those who write them.

"Our second area of activity," Massimo continues, "is related to education and scientific research. The Foundation provides direct aid to The Caravan, the school that Enzo founded with some friends in Modena in 1979. We also provide scholarships allowing young medical students to do their specializations at the various international centers of excellence with which Enzo had ties. Finally, we support research projects including the early diagnosis of tumors that had commenced thanks to one of our great friend's insights."

Enzo's tomb in the small cemetery of Cittanova, near Modena, is made of white marble, with the upper portion leaning, as a reminder of the stone rolled away from Christ's tomb on the day of his resurrection and his victory over death. It has become the site of continuous visits.

Young people who never knew Enzo but who look to him as a teacher also come. On his white tomb they find the words, "In the simplicity of my heart I have gladly given you everything."

That seed planted in Emilian soil is also bearing fruit abroad. Among the testimonies gathered by the Enzo Piccinini Foundation is that of Claudia, from South America.

"My encounter with Enzo was a gratuitous gift, and he has proven to be a greater and greater friend in my life. I was in a time of great sadness and disappointment. I was incapable of overcoming my negative outlook."

Claudia heard about Enzo and felt curious to get to know him. She found a pamphlet with his witness, entitled "Thinking 'You Alone, O Ideal, Are True.'"

"I started reading it right away, and as I read, I became more and more surprised. The love that Enzo had for life and his capacity for dedication to others struck me.

"Words like wonder, event, encounter, companionship, friendship, offering, that I had often heard spoken in an impersonal way, began to take on life: the experience lived by a person whose life was a gift for Someone else and for others. The words took on a face, the face of Piccinini, who introduced himself as a witness to a life that corresponded to the needs I was feeling in my heart.

"After reading Enzo's testimony, I started reading Father Luigi Giussani's books, and to my surprise I understood his words. What I was reading found an application in my life, and what I was living found an answer in what I read. I started to feel like Father Giussani's daughter. I believe that Enzo drew me close to him, and Father Giussani in turn drew me close to Christ and his Church.

"I dare to say that Enzo has begotten me and shown me the one who had begotten him, leading to the Source of sources, namely, Christ."

Historical Information

Enzo Piccinini was born in Scandiano within the municipality of Reggio Emilia on June 5, 1951. In 1970 he graduated with a classical education from the Rinaldini public gymnasium lyceum in Ancona, and in 1971 he enrolled in the College of Medicine and Surgery at the University of Modena. He took part in the Communion and Liberation movement, which was taking its first steps in Italian universities at that time.

In 1973 he married Fiorisa Manzotti, and around the same time he formed a close personal relationship with Father Luigi Giussani, founder of the Movement of Communion and Liberation. In 1976 he graduated with a degree in medicine and surgery, and began a specialization first in general surgery and later in vascular surgery. In 1979, as his eldest daughter was about to begin elementary school, his awareness of the importance of a clear educational proposal developed. Enzo suggested to some of his friends the idea of establishing a school in Modena directly managed by a cooperative of parents and teachers. On May 2, 1979, the cooperative known as The Caravan was founded, with Piccinini guiding every important decision.

At the same time, with another group of friends, he created a cultural center which in 1979 took the name of "Poetry Hill Cultural Center."[1] In 1980 he transferred to the University of Bologna.

In his professional life, Piccinini always made it a priority to unite his clinical activity with research and teaching, which included maintaining ties with the most qualified university centers of excellence, with whom he collaborated on several research projects, including Harvard University, the University of Chicago and the Pierre and Marie Curie University of Paris. In 1999, Doctor Piccinini was responsible for creating a masters program in coloproctology, sponsored by the European Union and the University of Bologna, in collaboration with the Universities of Vienna and Madrid.

On May 26, 1999, Enzo Piccinini died in a car accident near Fidenza on the A1 freeway. His funeral, celebrated by Cardinal Giacomo Biffi in the Basilica of San Petronio in Bologna, was attended by more than seven thousand people.

---

1. In Italian: "Centro Culturale La Collina della Poesia."

The Enzo Piccinini Foundation

In December of 2002, in order to continue the ideals to which Enzo Piccinini was committed, a foundation that bears his name was established.

The Foundation supports and promotes works that testify to the beauty that was met and lived with Enzo. It engages in three areas of activity, in keeping with the major interests that animated Piccinini's existence: 1) education and training; 2) scientific research and preparation for the medical profession; 3) culture and documentation.

Educational and training area

The Foundation supports projects aimed at educating and training children and young people through the establishment and management of schools, training courses, and residential or semi-residential structures for students.

An initial large project has already been completed, with the acquisition of a five-acre plot and support for the construction of a new school building for The Caravan in Modena. In 1979, Enzo was the first director, in the Emilian town where he lived, of the first school run by The Caravan cooperative. In later years, he supported its work and its development.

The cornerstone was laid on May 26, 2003. The completion of the project was celebrated on May 26, 2005. In September of that year, The Caravan reopened its doors in its new modern structure that houses classes from preschool to the first year of secondary school.

Scientific and medical area

Following what was begun and suggested by Enzo, and in collaboration with national and international academic centers, several research projects have begun in the field of cancer surgery and the study of molecular biology, producing scientific publications which have appeared in authoritative international journals.

Since June of 2005, there has been active cooperation between the Piccinini Foundation, the Elio Bisulli Foundation of Cesena, and the Department of

Histology, Embryology and Applied Biology of the University of Bologna to carry out research initiatives with the following goals: 1) the study of neoplastic diseases, with particular attention to colorectal cancer; 2) research on the early molecular markers of human diseases; 3) the study of the molecular physiology and pathophysiology of human epithelial tissues.

The Foundation also awards scholarships to enable young undergraduates and graduates in medicine and surgery to attend centers of excellence in Italy and abroad, with which Enzo had established relations, in order to refine their skills in the practice of clinical medicine. Update courses for surgeons with a specific interest in surgery for cancer of the digestive system are also offered.

Historical and cultural area

The Foundation, through a proprietary informational archive, is engaged in researching, sorting, cataloguing, preserving and repairing documents, writings, letters, and testimonies related to Enzo's life and work.

The Foundation also promotes and supports exhibitions, conferences, and publishing projects to introduce Piccinini to the world and to show how his memory continues to generate relationships, initiatives and activities.

To facilitate the collection of this documentation, the Foundations seeks input from those who have writings, letters, recordings, films, and testimonies related to the life of Enzo Piccinini. Those who have such items in their possession are invited to send them or copies of them to the Archives, even if only temporarily

The address of the Enzo Piccinini Foundation Archives, where documents and testimonials can be sent, is
Via del Carpentiere n. 30, 40138 Bologna, Italy.
    For further information:
    Telephone: (39) 051-533883
    Email: archivio@fondazionepiccinini.org

How to support the Foundation

You can give concrete support to the development of the projects of the Enzo Piccinini Foundation in the following ways:
– Ongoing annual support
– Freewill gifts
– Sponsorship of scheduled events
– Donations and bequests

Data for bank transfers:

Account number 8723512 at the Unicredit Banca, Modena Morane office
Payable to the Enzo Piccinini Foundation

International Bank Account Number (IBAN):
IT39L0200812906000008723512

Website

Further information and news about the activities of the Foundation, together with documents and texts concerning the life and work of Enzo Piccinini, can be found at www.fondazionepiccinini.org.

Enrollment in the site makes it possible to receive updates about Foundation activities.

The Amistad Group

In addition to the Piccinini Foundation, the Amistad Group is also committed to raise awareness and deepen the legacy of Enzo.

The Amistad Group was founded in early 2000 at the suggestion of Sister Anna Minghetti. She invited several families to sponsor children from the area of Humocaro in Venezuela, where one of Enzo's sisters works as a nun, as a way of witnessing to the memory of the immense gift of friendship received from him.

Distance sponsorship is an ongoing activity which includes not only making an annual contribution, but also involves a commitment to a relationship with the children and their families, so that over time they may recognize that a selfless gift has impacted the drama of their lives and, more deeply, has awakened trust and hope in them.

In addition to its other activities of solidarity, the Amistad Group also promotes meetings for the purpose of introducing Enzo to others, inviting speakers who knew him.

The Amistad Group also contributes to the pediatric medical center Angel de la Guarda, as a part of the "Adopt a Work" program of AVSI, which includes the operation of its educational center and the operation of the dental surgery clinic dedicated to Matteo Candini.

Further information can be obtained by visiting the site www.gruppoamistad.it or by writing to info@gruppoamistad.it.

Acknowledgements

Thanks go to the following for their contributions to this text:

Ilde Ferretti
Fiorisa Manzotti
Anna Rita Piccinini
Pietro Piccinini
Maria Piccinini
Chiara Piccinini
Stefano Alberto (Father Pino)
Lodovico Balducci
Pier Paolo Bellini (Widmer)
Luigi Benatti
Nadia Bertelli
Raffaele Bisulli
Carlo Caffarra
Giancarlo Cesana
Graziano Debellini
Davide Donati
Mario Dupuis
Susanna Marroccu
Carla Morelli
Massimo Moscatelli
Luigi Negri
Giuseppe Ranalli
Cristina Rossi
Alberto Savorana
Pierluigi Strippoli
Elena Ugolini
Giampaolo Ugolini
Massimo Vincenzi
Giorgio Vittadini

www.ingramcontent.com/pod-product-compliance
Lightning Source LLC
Chambersburg PA
CBHW070647300426
44111CB00013B/2312